RULE
BREAKER
INVESTING

RULE
BREAKER
INVESTING

How to Pick the
BEST STOCKS
of the Future and Build
LASTING WEALTH

David Gardner

Harriman House

HARRIMAN HOUSE LTD
Website: harriman.house

First published in 2025 by Harriman House, an imprint of Pan Macmillan
Associated companies throughout the world
www.panmacmillan.com

Copyright © David Gardner 2025

The right of David Gardner to be identified as the author has been asserted in accordance with
the Copyright, Design and Patents Act 1988.

Hardback ISBN: 978-1-80409-121-0
eBook ISBN: 978-1-80409-122-7

01

Printed in the United States of America.

Cover design by Christopher Parker.

**"Fool," said my Muse to me.
"Look in thy heart and write."**

—SIR PHILIP SIDNEY

The best books come from someplace inside.
You don't write because you want to, but because you have to.

—JUDY BLUME

The person who writes for Fools is always sure of a large audience.

—ARTHUR SCHOPENHAUER

EVERYONE IS AN INVESTOR.

When addressing a room, I've said, "Raise your hand if you're an investor." It's a trick question; it catches only those who think investing is what *other* people do. A specialized class. Not me or you, right? Wrong.

Put your hand up.

Everyone is an investor, of both money and time. Your choice to do *this*, not that... to spend here, not there... are all **investments**. Even starting out with little money, you have as much time in a day as anyone else. And using time as your money's greatest ally is one thing I'm here to help you do.

Everyone is an investor, and everyone can make a 100-bagger! By that, I mean you can invest money in a company that will grow 100 times or more. I know because I've done it myself; I've written this book to help you do the same.

For decades, I've provided investing advice for millions of people via the company I helped found, The Motley Fool. When I retired from Motley Fool Stock Advisor, one of the world's largest investment advisory services, my stock-picking record had generated returns of 21% annualized over 20 years, vs. the S&P 500's return of 9%.

Those returns were powered by zigging as Wall Street zagged, challenging its conventional wisdoms and, most of all, by breaking the rules. The surest way to beat the market is to find the mega-winners of every era, and my returns have been powered by not one, but seven, 100-baggers.

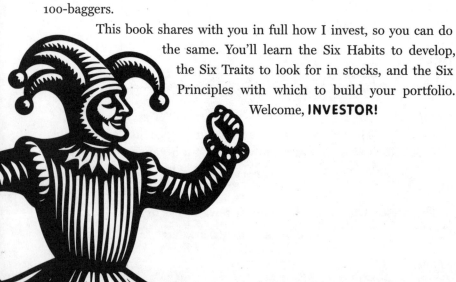

This book shares with you in full how I invest, so you can do the same. You'll learn the Six Habits to develop, the Six Traits to look for in stocks, and the Six Principles with which to build your portfolio. Welcome, **INVESTOR!**

CONTENTS

INTRODUCTION

LING'S MONEY THING

A BC'S LONG-RUNNING DAYTIME show *The View* had a brand new co-host. The year was 1998 and 25-year-old Lisa Ling had joined a cast of established stars like Barbara Walters and Meredith Vieira. The show's producers aimed to give Lisa some fun escapades, to take viewers on new adventures in learning. They thought: "The stock market."

So, at Motley Fool headquarters, we got an invitation to put on our jester caps and fly to New York City for "Ling's Money Thing."

The plan? "Let's have Lisa invest," suggested the producers. "Have her model good financial behavior for our viewers, pick a stock. But since Lisa's not a stockpicker herself, we'll invite you Fools on, and you'll pick a stock for Lisa.

"So guys, think of a stock, of a company that she would like, that fits with who she is. 'Buy what you know' is the idea."

We knew that idea well. I've loved it ever since Peter Lynch popularized it in the 1980s in *One Up on Wall Street*, a book that switched me on to investing.

We scored a phone interview with Lisa: What brands did she wear? What were her hobbies? "When you open up your fridge, Lisa," we asked, "what makes you smile?"

"We" were my brother Tom and I, co-founders of The Motley Fool, which had launched on America Online (AOL) four years earlier. We'd been on the cover of *Fortune* and written a couple of bestsellers encouraging individual stock picking. Our enthusiastic willingness to wear motley (multi-colored) Fool's caps in public probably didn't hurt our chances of being invited on shows like this, especially since we were closer in age to Lisa than to Barbara Walters.

"It was a good conversation, guys. Lisa enjoyed meeting you. Come up to New York for the show next week. **Do you have the stock?**"

"We've talked about it. Yes. We have the stock."

"Great. See you Thursday."

Thursday, July 2, 1998, marked the first of our two historic appearances on *The View*. "Ling's Money Thing" was about to get real.

Tom and I arrived for the taping, standing off-stage in the wings, readying ourselves for the live studio audience. It began:

"The Motley Fools are here!" The studio audience cheered. (If you've ever been in a live TV talk show audience, you know it's your job to cheer.) "Lisa's going to pick a stock! And they're here to help her do it. Please welcome David and Tom Gardner!" We had our jester caps on, our stock pick ready, and some lively on-air banter cued up for the hosts.

Then it was time to talk stocks, and we made our pick. The studio audience seemed to approve, and Lisa was in on it from the start, already briefed on our selection. The segment moved along smoothly for the next five or six minutes. We jogged off the set to hear the producer exclaim, "Great job, guys. Really. Let's have you back. Let's update the story."

Over the next six weeks the stock lost 33% of its value.

By the time they had us back on the show, a full third of "Lisa's money" was gone. And we were OK talking about that; I like to talk about my losers—there's never been a shortage. (I'll do that in this book, too.)

August 16, 1998 marked our second—and to date, final—historic appearance on *The View*.

Once again, a live studio audience, their energy buzzing like a hive. "Here come the guys! They're back to talk about Lisa's stock." Lisa was smiling, looking excited. She knew where we were headed with this. She was a good sport.

As we started to talk about what had happened over those six weeks, our expressions turned crestfallen. The segment went something like this:

"Hey, everybody. The Motley Fools are back. It's Ling's Money Thing!"

Yay! Cheers! Cheers!

"And they've got an *update* on the stock for Lisa."

More cheers.

"And that stock is... down!"

And at that point—well, a friend of ours who's watched *The View* from time to time told us, "You know, guys, I think you're the only ones I've ever seen actually booed on *The View*."

Yes, the audience gave us a good-natured, loud boo when we revealed that Lisa's fantasy portfolio had dropped by 33%.

In the few minutes we had, we explained that the company itself was fine, but a July earnings call had spooked investors when the CEO mentioned being more comfortable with "the lower end" of future estimates. That led to a 14% drop in one day, and the shares continued to slip. But we stressed our long-term commitment.

Now, about The Stock....

The stock we picked for Ling's Money Thing in July of 1998 was **Starbucks** (SBUX). Starbucks was our pick for Lisa.

Starbucks had a tough summer in 1998, with one disappointing earnings report—not due to poor performance, but because CEO Howard Schultz conservatively underpromised on future results. Underpromised, but he would wind up overdelivering: By the following summer, Starbucks not only fully recovered, but was up 40% overall!

But we never got to share that. No further invitation followed, no cheering studio audience ever reconvened. "Ling's Money Thing" fizzled out like yesterday's cappuccino foam.

One thing kept going, though... Starbucks.

THE "IT WAS... ... ... STARBUCKS!" LESSON

While Lisa's Starbucks stock was fantasy money, the lesson is real. And with time, it only grows more powerful when we see compounding at work with great stocks to hold like Starbucks... if you actually *do* hold. And hold, and hold. Which is what I do. And I hope you will too after finishing Part I of this book!

On the day we appeared on *The View*, Starbucks opened at $42 a share. Since then, the stock has split 2-for-1 four times. While traditional stock splits are overrated non-events, they have a real impact by multiplying the number of shares held each time, proportionately reducing the share price.

So, shareholders (Lisa...?) who've held on since summer 1998 now have 16 shares for every one they originally owned. That $42 price tag back then is now effectively $2.63 today (the "split-adjusted price").

So yeah, we picked Starbucks for Lisa at $2.63, and as this book went to press, Starbucks was trading at $91.25. That's a 3,370% increase, 34 times in value![1] The broader market, as measured by the S&P 500 with dividends reinvested, has risen 700% over the same period. Not bad... but maybe you can see why I prefer stocks over index funds?

Since we never did get invited back on the show, *The View*'s audience has missed this part. Starbucks has seen its ups and downs since 1998, but like the stocks in Part II, it's been *up a lot more than down.*

Today, Starbucks is valued at over $100 billion. Over the past two-plus decades, patient shareholders who have bought, *held*, and maybe even added to Starbucks stock have had front-row seats to an object lesson in what investing really is, and means. Lucrative front-row seats. This book will show you how to find and stay in those seats.

HELLO (AGAIN), WORLD

I'm David Gardner. Since the mid-1990s, from the dawn of the internet to its rise as the dominant technology of our time, I've pursued something radical: beating the stock market averages and teaching the world how to do the same.

I've picked stocks, one at a time, month by month, and fully scored every hit and miss with complete transparency. Every home run (we'll talk about those) and strikeout (those too) is documented and available for review. I've consistently and spectacularly outperformed using my Rule Breaker Investing strategy.

As co-chairman and co-founder of The Motley Fool, I stepped back from stock picking in May 2021 and spent the past few years organizing

---

1 These returns don't include reinvested dividends. Starbucks has paid dividends since April 2010.

hundreds of notes: stories, lessons, performance numbers, and all manner of "Rule Breaker-y thoughts."

I can't wait to get started.

In the past, getting started meant STOCK PICKS.

What did people hope for, listening to our Motley Fool Radio Show on National Public Radio? What did late-night browsers, scrolling through Fool articles after a long day just hoping to uncover the next big opportunity, *really* want to find? What's been the common request at every investor conference, seminar, or webinar during Q&A?

Stock picks.

And not just the picks, but the reasoning behind them. That's how our business began. We've always delivered stock picks.

What did Lisa Ling and *The View* want? (Take a wild guess.)

But, what did Lisa Ling, the producers, her audience, and the world beyond *actually need*?

They needed to know how to behave, to develop better habits built upon winning foundations.

Because if I pick—oh I dunno... say, *Starbucks*—and it has a bad six weeks, and we just up and quit (sell the stock... heck, just *end this Money Thing*!), then even the greatest stock picks in the world won't amount to a hill of coffee beans.

The world may want stock picks, and believe me I have given 'em, but if people aren't *behaving* with these picks in a way that will make them money, it makes one want to say, in the words of Austin Powers, "Oh, *behave!*"

And so here's how I have organized this book....

WHAT TO EXPECT FROM THIS BOOK

This book is organized in three parts, with a bonus Chapter O at the start—a playful "optional" chapter placed strategically before Part I. Think of Chapter O as your invitation to rethink what you believe you already know about investing, and perhaps even about yourself. It's a mindset-reset, designed to prepare you for what's ahead.

And then we get to Part I.

Part I features the 6 Habits of the Rule Breaker Investor

Which stocks to pick and why are critical material, but there's something more valuable I can give you first. An answer to this question:

What is the right mindset, what are the right habits, for me to achieve outstanding success as an investor?

If you walk away from this book with a self-confident answer to this question alone, nothing else matters so much!

Part I invites you into the delightful chaos of investing, where we'll tackle everything from why great stocks sometimes stumble to why math and biology conspire to make us bad at it. We'll explore why "Buy Low, Sell High" is the bumper sticker of missed opportunities, how to embrace market dips, and the thrill of putting on your investment jersey for the wild rollercoaster ahead.

You'll also discover why purpose beats profit every time, and why investing in at least 20 stocks (yes, 20!) keeps you winning, even when the market swings like Babe Ruth.

Part II features the 6 Traits of the Rule Breaker Stock

This is the beating heart of the book, wherein I answer:

What traits define the greatest stocks, the Rule Breakers, of every era?

In Part II, we'll dive deeper into the stocks that stand the test of time—starting with the quirky yet telling "Snap Cola Test" and why seeing through dark clouds can give you an edge. We'll explore the ones that got away, the art of spotting sustainable competitive advantages, and why no single trait of a stock can carry it alone—it's a concert!

Plus, you'll learn what toothpaste can teach us about strong consumer appeal, how to judge good management, and why being "overvalued" may just be the market's biggest inside joke.

The right mindset (Part I) and the right stocks (Part II) naturally call into being a third thing, a portfolio... *yours.* Most people don't have any coaching for how to build one. The most common question from new listeners of my Rule Breaker Investing podcast is: *"What's the right number of stocks for my portfolio?"* (Hint: No such number. We'll talk about this later.)

Part III features the 6 Principles of the Rule Breaker Portfolio

This is the part that brings it all together—it's about your portfolio, after all! Here I'll aim to provide you with the grounding most people lack, answering:

What are the principles by which I will build and manage my portfolio?

In Part III, we'll pull everything together as you craft a portfolio that reflects your best vision for the future—complete with multiple futures, applying Henrik's T-Shirt Test. We'll name the purpose behind your investments, grow your circle of competence, and show you how to buy in thirds. Then, it's time to establish your "sleep number"—back your thoroughbreds, retire your also-rans, and explore the myth of rebalancing. Finally, we'll see why investing is a full race, not a sprint, introducing a Five-and-Three framework that makes time management your secret weapon.

A greatest-hits list of key lessons awaits you in Things to Remember at the end of the book, as well as a Glossary designed to educate, to amuse, and to enrich.

Then you'll be ready to open up a can of...

SPIFFY-POP!

It's the Holy Grail of investment success. *The Spiffy-Pop.* Yet most people never experience one for 18 reasons.

They *haven't* formed winning Habits. (Six of them.)

They *don't* buy stocks possessing the right Traits. (Six of those, too.)

They *don't* set up their portfolio with solid Principles. (Guess how many?)

But wait, why am I talking spiffy-pops when you probably don't even know what they are yet? (Keep reading.)

Covering how you should invest (the Habits), what to invest in (the Traits), *and* how to oversee a portfolio (the Principles) is ambitious. Each of these could fill a book on its own. But by integrating them together in just this one short book, I'm hoping the lessons and results may be even more powerful. It's worth a shot!

Let's go for it.

CHAPTER O

LAYING THE GROUNDWORK

G O AHEAD. SKIP this chapter. It's Chapter Zero, after all.

When I shared the first draft of this book, half of my early readers (let's call them group one) were all about: "Just get on with it! I read the intro. Give me Chapter 1 and the first Rule Breaker Habit." These readers knew my podcast, track record, and the whole idea of jesters and Foolishness challenging conventional wisdom. They were already Rule Breakers. They wanted Chapter 1, not Chapter Zero.

Group two wasn't as familiar. To them, Rule-Breaking sounded like something you're taught *not* to do. Plus, isn't there that saying that "fools and their money are soon parted"? Why read this book? What's it even about?

So this chapter is a welcome mat for those (group two) who'd like one. Most every other book starts with Chapter 1, but this isn't every other book. And hey, zero *is* a number, and the Fool and Rule Breaker in me always wanted to do this.[2] Zero can be read as a number, but it can also be read as a letter:

Chapter O, where "O" is for optional—a short course in Foolishness *only* for those interested. (Otherwise, see you at Chapter One.)

---

2 It also helps ensure a symmetrical table of contents, as I knew near the end I'd write a Chapter X!

YOUR PARENTS WERE WRONG

Mine were too, by the way.

Growing up, I often heard this after lunch on many a summer day:

"Hey kids, you have to stay out of the pool for 30 minutes to let your food digest."

The idea was that swimming right after eating could cause cramps, which could lead to drowning. There's little scientific evidence to support this; you can swim just fine on a full stomach. This was wrong.

More examples of wrong things I heard from family or others while growing up:

- Eating carrots improves your (night) vision.
- We use only 10% of our brains.
- Reading in dim light ruins your eyesight.
- Swallowed chewing gum stays in your stomach for seven years.
- You'll catch a cold from cold weather.

Subsequent studies—otherwise known as science—have disproved every one of these myths. Every single one is wrong. Yet, throughout much of my younger life, I heard them repeatedly from authority figures and believed them to be true.

What's my point?

I'm here to prepare you for *rethinking* your relationship with money and what works in investing. Because just as these received "wisdoms" became conventional, so too have countless mistaken notions about investing. As we move forward in this book, I plan to topple more towers of tradition. I want you to recognize that many things you may have heard before about the stock market—that it's too risky for the average person— that to do better than the market averages or index funds is just luck— that timing the market is key to success—are, to me, dogmas begging to be discredited. I'll happily do just that.

So by reminding you that oft-repeated claims like "swallowed chewing gum stays in your stomach for seven years" or "we use only 10% of our brains" are fundamentally untrue, I hope to show that Breaking the Rules is not just more fun (it is)—but downright necessary to win, and win big. For instance, shortly I will be shooting "buy low, sell high" full of holes.

When people are convinced something is true and it turns out to be false, those who thought differently achieve the greatest wins. This pattern will come up repeatedly in this book.

I've experienced it firsthand. In the 1990s, I promoted what seemed like a radical message at the time: "People *will* use their credit cards over the internet." Back then, conventional wisdom said e-commerce would fail because people wouldn't be comfortable sharing their credit card numbers online. A related belief was that eBay would never work, because, "How can you trust a random person to send you what you paid for (assuming you were crazy enough to use your credit card on the internet)?!" eBay turned out to be a pretty great stock pick for me.

... AND SO WERE THEIR FINANCIAL ADVISORS

Not only were your parents wrong, but so were many of their financial advisors.

In one such example, David Northway shared the struggles of his earlier financial life on the Motley Fool message boards.

David had bought his first stock in college in the early 1970s, back when trading and commission fees were over $100. As he and his partner became more serious about their financial future, David invested in several mutual funds through dollar-cost-averaging, while she bought individual stocks like Apple, Microsoft, Nike, and Pepsi.

"As soon as they showed any profit," David wrote, "our broker convinced us to sell. 'Lock in profits' was his mantra." (Pocketing his sales commission... cough, cough.)

Years later, David calculated that those combined positions would today be worth "north of $10 million."

"Once we realized our mistakes with a regular broker, we sought out a financial manager. One who came heavily recommended was engaged in actively moving funds back and forth between a money-market fund and a large-cap fund based on his secret set of signals and calculations. Sometimes these exchanges between funds happened multiple times a day. We stayed with him for about two years until he was charged with fraud and lost his license. The silver lining was that he did have our remaining funds invested in two different large-cap mutual funds which we left alone after his arrest and they continued to do well, far better in fact than his market-timing approach (duh!).

"We next used a man who had been named one of *Barron's* top ten up-and-coming financial managers of the year. Although now this may seem impossible to believe, he based his market-timing approach on his PhD dissertation that was a study of chaos theory and the movement of sea slugs. It does make me smile when I think of it looking back. Not surprisingly he produced almost no results for several years before we abandoned him. At least *he* didn't commit fraud.

"Next, one of our good friends, and the father of one of our daughter's best friends, started an investment business. Many of our group of friends invested heavily in his private 'Momo' (for momentum) fund. He produced monthly reports of how well we were doing and our investments seemed to be growing regularly. However at the end of his second year of running the fund he held a meeting of all the fund owners and announced he had a serious gambling problem and had actually lost all the invested money. He pleaded with us not to turn him into the police, and painted a picture of his daughter (our daughter's good friend) going without a father while he served time in prison. While this fraud was going on, fortunately we continued to invest regularly in mutual funds and wisely did not transfer all those assets to the charlatan.

"Finally in the early 2000s after suffering through the dotcom bust and seeing even our mutual funds take a big hit, I started reading commentary and seeing information about The Motley Fool." And the rest, for him, has been history (of the good kind).

Not every financial advisor was corrupt or inept back then. Some of my best friends were brokers. But the system was hit-and-miss, and in many ways, it was corrupted at its core. When Tom and I first put on our Fool caps on CNBC in the mid-1990s, we were seen as radicals, pushing back against a financial industry where brokers were incentivized by commissions to get you to trade, and managed mutual funds extracted ridiculous front-end "load" fees, additionally raking too much off the top every year afterward. "Index funds beat mutual funds"—one of our members was an opera performer and cut a song with those lyrics that we would replay on our NPR show.

Here's my longest sentence of the book (apologies ahead of time, but it just feels right to deliver this in one mouthful):

> Even though we disagreed on one key point with Jack Bogle, the founder of both Vanguard and of the index-fund revolution—that individual investors should not (he said) buy individual stocks (we say you should!)—we dearly loved Jack as a person and what he stood for and did in this world, which was to help wipe it of bad advisors and the compensation systems that drove those people because of overpriced, opaque schemes (Ponzi, but others too) that were enabled by a status quo where the average person wasn't educated about money, and thus as an adult was walking into a red-light district of financial choices where even some of the cops couldn't be trusted.

Your parents may have been wrong (sometimes) but often innocently so, and they loved you. Your financial professionals—the worst ones— were knowingly wrong... and they only loved your money.

EVERY $ AROUND YOU IS $64

Let's talk more about money—and recognize two key truths about it.

First, it loses value over time. That's the bad news. The reason your great-grandfather's $1 from 1925 was so valuable is that its purchasing power was far greater than it sounds: $1 back then is equivalent to $17 today. Most governments print new money every year, increasing the money supply and causing each dollar gradually to lose value. It's called inflation, and I know you know that. Most people do.

The second truth is less commonly known: When invested, money compounds and can grow exponentially. When invested well, it compounds at a rate well in excess of inflation. The stock market has historically returned about 10% annually. This means, on average, that money invested in the market doubles every seven years.

Once you recognize that, it really changes how you view $1! For me, I like to think forward 42 years, which allows that seven-year double to happen six times. What does that mean? It means every dollar bill you're holding, or spending at Starbucks, or investing today *is actually worth $64* to your future self.[3]

Here's one of those "put everyone in the world into just two buckets" propositions: There are two types of people in this world, those who raise their hands recognizing they are investors and treat every dollar like it's $64, and those who don't. If you haven't yet awakened to this, I hope this helps you do so.

PERSONAL FINANCE IN ONE PAGE

Being a good steward of your personal finances is what enables successful stock market investing! This is an investment book, not a personal finance guide, so little ink will be spilled on personal finance basics, but I need briefly to shout out their foundational role.

Forget about a whole page. Here's a line:

I urge you to live below your means every day of your life.

That habit enables financial resilience and long-term wealth-building. Without it, even the best investments won't save you from financial stress. And I absolutely insist you eliminate any double-digit-interest-rate credit card debt before buying stocks!

These basics are essential to cultivating the garden that is your investment portfolio, which nurtures your financial life. So ensure that what you plant has an unimpeded opportunity to grow through storms and dry seasons. Uprooting investments because you didn't build an emergency fund is a tragic mistake.

---

3 I chose 42 years because I've always liked that number, ever since discovering from Douglas Adams that it is the answer to the ultimate question of life, the universe, and everything. Plus, as I started to write this book, in 42 years I would be 100. (I hope you'll live even longer.) Pick whatever number you like.

Chapter O

There are many good books on personal finance... or just consult the internet or AI! Reliable, well-trafficked, free financial sites and apps are your friends. Three top ones for advice:

1. The Motley Fool (www.fool.com)
2. NerdWallet (www.nerdwallet.com)
3. Investopedia (www.investopedia.com)

We live in an info-abundant age. With the basics in place, you'll be ready to plant wisely and watch your garden grow.

MACROECONOMICS

Even with their personal finances in working order, I imagine some people don't invest because they're intimidated by stories like these:

"The Fed is Needlessly Delaying Rate Cuts"

"Stocks Drop and Treasury Yields Jump as Inflation Data Shakes Rate Bets"

"Stocks and Bonds Diverge as Investors Worry Less about Inflation"

"Goldman: The US GDP–GDI Gap Won't Hurt You"

These are real headlines drawn just from one financial newspaper, on the very morning I wrote this. There were plenty more.

The implication of such headlines is twofold, and neither is good: (1) You probably don't understand all these terms (*didn't you major in economics?!*), so maybe you should never buy stocks, and (2) even if you do understand some or all of these terms, do you have an intelligent, developed viewpoint on each topic? *Is your viewpoint correct?* If not, you should probably never buy stocks.

Macroeconomics, the study of economy-wide phenomena, is a great subject. Understanding *basic economics* (Thomas Sowell titled a masterwork on this) is incredibly useful in life. Concepts like supply and demand, and "there's no free lunch," are timeless principles that will always hold true and are important to grasp.

But when we start talking about where interest rates will be next autumn, or whether a particular currency is going to fluctuate, or the future price of oil... we're venturing into territory you don't need to spend any time on—at least, not if you invest like me, as I convey in this book. The primary reason is that almost all "macro talk" focuses on—sometimes obsesses over—near-term conditions. It's fodder for experts debating where we are in any given cycle. Let the pundits have their airtime (I don't watch financial TV).

Our truth is that as we pick stocks and build out our portfolios, it's like we're stringing together cars on a train. As Rule Breaker investors, you and I are getting on that train. The track is laid, and we're staying on that train *all the way across the country*. The train will keep most, if not all, of its cars (we might let go of the caboose) from start to finish. The weather (the macro picture) will change constantly as we journey across the country! It's a long trip together. Being overfocused on whether it'll snow as we approach St. Louis or trying to forecast the temperature as we'll chug through Arizona is of no consequence *compared to the destination we seek*. I'm much more interested in the train than the weather, but I'm even more interested in the destination than the train.

That's my way of saying that *investing* persistently your whole life long is so much more important than today's macroeconomic headlines. Those who avoid investing because they're intimidated by macroeconomics, or by some forecast encountered while doom-scrolling, are severely undermining their financial futures.

Here's a quote for you:

Forming macro opinions or listening to the macro or market predictions of others is a waste of time.

... what rapscallion would say such a thing?!
Warren Buffett.

Chapter 0

WHY WE BREAK THE RULES

It took years for me to articulate what started as intuition and eventually evolved into this question:

Why do the most esteemed investment books of the past often cause their readers to miss the best stocks of their own generation?

I won't claim it's true of every revered book, but it's strikingly true for many. Devotees of a classic like *The Intelligent Investor* likely wouldn't have picked Starbucks in 1998... or Amazon in 1997, Tesla in 2011, Netflix in 2004, or Nvidia in 2005—the years I picked these stocks, and I'm still holding.

Even Warren Buffett, whom I consider the greatest American investor, didn't pick these stocks then—or for the most part, ever after.

And yet they're among the truly great stocks of this past generation.

The answer to the question above is that well-reasoned thoughts and assumptions can be taken too far. They can become gospel, morph into conventional wisdom which is taught, proliferates, becomes *the way things are done around here*. These notions become Rules.

Part of my success, and that of those who've followed me for three decades, is rooted in playing David to the Goliaths—to books like *The Intelligent Investor* and attention-magnets like Warren Buffett (again, deservedly so). Goliaths set the Rules, shaping the world with their powerful constructs. Much like a quote gains weight when attributed to Lincoln or Churchill, anything said in the name of Buffett, "value investing," or Benjamin Graham becomes a Rule. And academia teaches and reinforces these Rules.

But as Malcolm Gladwell argues in *How David Beats Goliath*, if you compete with Goliath by playing by his Rules, you'll lose. The only way to win is, like David, to *break* the rules. To take the road less traveled. Or put another way: to play the Fool in a world of Wise Men. That's how David beats Goliath.

The key to Rule Breaker Investing's success is that its Habits, Traits, and Principles subvert the conventional wisdom. In this sense, I had to have Buffett be the amazing investor that Buffett is in order to set the narrative *so* convincingly for *so* many that, for a generation now, they have mistrusted and avoided "overvalued" stocks with high price-to-earnings ratios, with gaudy-looking past performance, birthing risky new technologies.

Yet, these are the very stocks that have topped the lists of my own—and the world's—best performers since the year 2000. We'll explore this more later. I hope you get the point.

The point is to break the [bleeping] rules.

Okay, and *now*... Chapter 1.

PART

THE 6 HABITS OF THE RULE BREAKER INVESTOR

I DON'T REMEMBER a lot from fourth grade, but **one thing I will never forget.**

Mr. Hoskinson, a home-room teacher at St. Albans School in Washington, DC, took it upon himself to teach us the stock market.

Back then, you found stock prices in newspapers, quoted in fractions, not decimals. Mr. Hoskinson made it a contest: Each student picked a 10-stock portfolio to be scored over a few months. Every Thursday for weeks, we spent the same hour after lunch opening up the Business section of *The Washington Post*, looking up the prices of our 10 stocks, recording in pencil, line-by-line, on graph paper. More fun than grammar!

Time ran out. The contest ended. We turned in our ledgers with stock prices painstakingly scratched out in our best penmanship. He calculated the final results. There were about 25 kids in the class. I won! (Okay, well actually, my dad won. He picked all my stocks.)

What I'll never forget was my prize: A *hugely* oversized HERSHEY'S chocolate bar. Wonka-tastic. Best prize ever. Thank you, Mr. Hoskinson!

From early days, I was inspired by my elders to study, follow, and figure out stocks. Years later, our dad would give us not just stock picks, but stock savvy and our own portfolios. **I learned to build habits**, and habits are what Part I is all about. Just like Mr. Hoskinson's chocolate bar, the rewards of good investing habits are sweet, and fun, and hugely oversized.

It's Part I of *Rule Breaker Investing*. Have a candy bar.

CHAPTER 1

RULE NUMBER ONE: LET YOUR WINNERS RUN. HIGH.

N VIDIA TELLS YOU all you need to know, if you will but listen....[4]

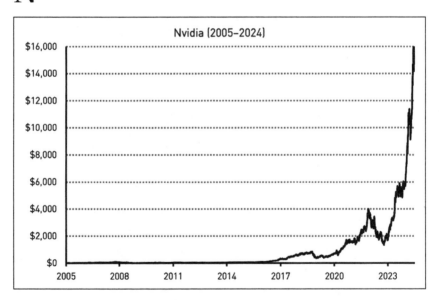

---

4 Nvidia has been a generationally great performer—one of the defining stock picks of my career. But it's important that you understand I'm not telling this story to showcase Nvidia itself. Volatile stock that it is, who knows where it will be in another six months, let alone six years? Time will tell. What I'm here to tell is that the habit of letting winners like Nvidia run, high, is the only way you'll ever make Rule Breaking investments in great stocks.

On April 15, 2005 (yep, Tax Day), Nvidia Corp. stock traded at $21.35 per share.

I know because that's the day I first picked it for Motley Fool Stock Advisor. Since then, it's been one of the great stocks of this (or any) era.

An out-and-out Rule Breaker, Nvidia exhibits all Six Traits we seek in a stock, which is why I picked it! More on that in Part II.

This chapter isn't about dissecting the stock; it's about building a habit, the first and probably the most important. *Without this habit*, you would have missed Nvidia, traded it too soon, stumbled, or let market noise shake you out—along with 99.9% of the investing world (mostly professionals). So you'd have missed out on the dreamy, world-beating, eye-popping, financial-freedom-making returns of a lifetime.

This chapter isn't about finding Nvidia. It's about holding onto it! We're here to develop the first habit of the Rule Breaker investor:

⋯→ RULE NUMBER ONE: ←⋯
LET YOUR WINNERS RUN. HIGH.

Let's follow the story of Nvidia....

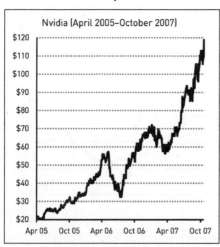

Nvidia (April 2005–October 2007)

By October 2007, the stock was making me look good, as it tipped the scales at $120. That's up about six times in value in two years—what we like to call a "six-bagger," in homage to Peter Lynch, who coined the "bagger" phrase.[5]

---

5 It's pulled from baseball. A home run in baseball is a "four-bagger." Lynch, a fellow baseball fan, pulled that into the investing world to colloquially refer to stocks that rise four times in value as "four-baggers." But "four" isn't what Lynch is famous for. He's famous for 10-baggers, which he held up as the big winners you want to aspire to. (You can't touch any more bases, or "bags," than four in baseball. In investing, you can go a *lot* further.)

But then came 2008. Those of you who were investing then, *do you remember 2008?* Nvidia dropped to $18! We went from riding high to looking really silly. The dang thing had been up six times in value, and now, three and a half years later, we were underwater.

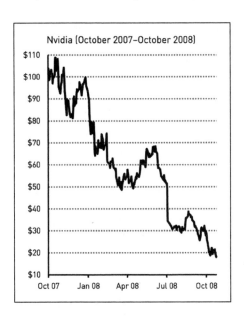

Nvidia (October 2007–October 2008)

By December 2009, Nvidia had begun to recover, and for my new monthly Motley Fool Stock Advisor pick (I picked one a month from 2002–2021), I re-recommended it. The stock was back to $50. "The timing is right," I wrote, "and so is the price. Nvidia just returned to profitability after three quarters in the red, and it has maintained a sterling balance sheet and strong cash flow. Analysts think Nvidia is on track to earn about $2.22 a share in fiscal 2011, which starts at the end of January. We think they're probably shooting too low.... Whether you're a Mac or a PC, you need Nvidia, and something that looks this sharp belongs in your portfolio."

[***record scratch***]

Let me interrupt the story briefly to ask: What exactly does "winner" mean here? Nvidia had shown extreme volatility, including an 80% drop in value while we were holding it! So, by what definition was Nvidia a winner, worth letting run?

Three factors: (1) Most importantly, *the business itself* generally continued to succeed and deliver, despite whatever the stock price was doing; (2) the stock price decline largely mirrored the overall market, which was abysmal in 2008, so Nvidia's volatility was in line with the broader market conditions; and, (3) by the time I re-recommended it,

Nvidia had more than doubled from $19.50 to $47, exhibiting what I call Habit #2. But I'm getting ahead of myself....

[***record scratch***]

Okay, five years later, at the end of 2014, the stock finally hit... $60. Yes, that bullish re-recommendation I made at $50 had only seen the stock rise 20% over five long years. It was still *just half of what it had been seven years earlier* ($60 in 2007), though it had now about tripled (a three-bagger) from our original 2005 cost basis.

Nvidia (Dec 2009–Dec 2014)

In 2016, Nvidia finally crossed $120, reclaiming that early high we'd celebrated in 2007, nine years earlier. Cue Jack Nicholson in *The Shining*: "We're baa-aaaack!"

By the end of that year, the stock had tripled again. Having started 2016 at $96, it closed at $319 and was far and away the top-performing stock on the S&P 500 (+198%). With our original $21.35 cost basis and that $50 re-entry, we were sitting a bit higher in the saddle.

I get dangerously Foolish urges from time to time, where I just *have* to challenge conventional wisdom and go further out on a limb to prove a big point. (Sometimes it works, sometimes it doesn't!) *Now* was one of those times. I thought about all my "regression to the mean" friends—people who say things like, "It's awfully expensive now!" or "What goes up must come down." You know, the ones who cite studies about how last year's top performers are bound to underperform next year.

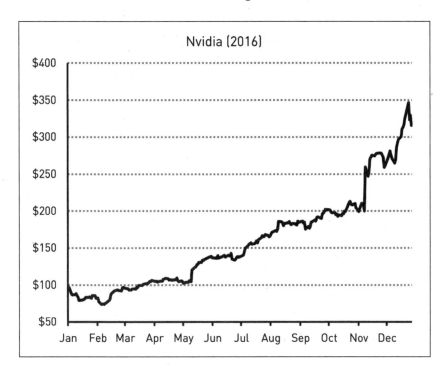

I recognize this *can be* true. But I love to point out when it's not, because (a) that'll shock some people, which is kind of fun, and (b) as I mentioned in Chapter O, when you're on the opposite side of conventional wisdom and you're right, while it's wrong, that's when you stand to make the most money.

So the very month after the media was buzzing about Nvidia being the top performer on the S&P 500 in 2016, in January 2017 I made Nvidia my *new* monthly recommendation for Motley Fool Stock Advisor (the third time it'd been my big monthly pick). I was showboating... and it worked. I wasn't picking Nvidia for just 2017 (you know me well enough by now to know that *we stay on the train*), but it was awfully nice to see it rise from our $307 recommendation price to $580 that year. Nvidia was the S&P 500's 10th top performer in 2017, up 83%.

I've never heard anyone follow "What goes up" with anything other than "must come down," but isn't that the point? When (a) *everyone* thinks that, and (b) we don't, and (c) they're wrong, then (d) whether or not their eyes are opened, (e) our eyes will likely take on the iconic $$ of Scrooge McDuck!

Because **with great Rule Breaker stocks, what goes up *ends up going upper*.** And that's why this first crucial Habit—letting your winners run, high—is so important.

To continue this remarkable story from 2005 to present: After running from $96 to $580 from 2016–2017, Nvidia touched *over $850* in 2018... but couldn't hold it and fell all the way down to—WHAMMO! (ouch)— $385. But by early 2020, it crossed back over $850 again. It ended 2020 at $1,560 (and yes, we're still sitting on our original cost of $21.35... now seeing the possibility of a 100-bagger move to $2,135).

Which, as it turns out, was actually shooting too low, because in 2021 the stock crossed $3,600!

Having started 2022 just over $3,600, shareholders watched their stock nosedive months later below $1,500, before closing the year cut in half, at $1,800. Nvidia, thy name is trombone: *Wah-wah-waaaaaaah!*

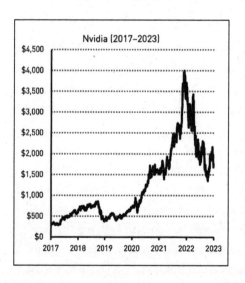

Nvidia (2017–2023)

Are you noticing how much we're recurrently losing? I hope so. Are you also noticing how much money we've made? Keep noticing.

Before we wrap up, let's take a moment to reflect on the staggering volatility Nvidia demonstrated at this scale. When a company as significant, large, and successful as Nvidia sees its stock price plummet from $3,600 to $1,800 in a single year, its market capitalization shrinks from $750 billion to $375 billion. Hundreds of billions of dollars, *poof,* all gone in a single year.[6] That's a striking example

---

6 That was nothing. On January 27, 2025, news of a Chinese AI rival, DeepSeek, sent Nvidia plunging 17%—erasing **$500 billion** in a single day, the largest one-day loss in market history. (*Poof!*)

of how *inefficient* markets can be—by which I mean certifiably crazy. Yes, crazy, but that doesn't mean there isn't a lot to learn from the Nvidia story.

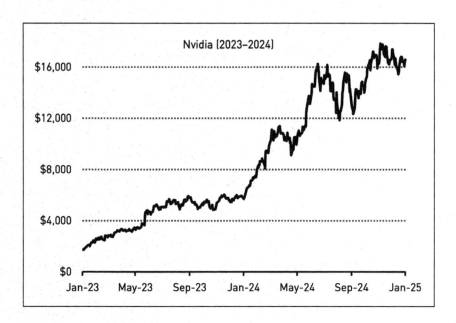

As this book went to press, Nvidia sat at $16,115 a share, proof positive of, well, a lot of things:

Proof positive, for one, that its pioneering role in GPU (Graphics Processing Unit) technology had become integral not just in gaming, where things started, but also in expanding fields like artificial intelligence, data centers, and autonomous vehicles. We'll dive deeper into these traits in Part II, where you'll learn why stocks like this are ones to let run.

Proof positive that the market is willing to bid Rule Breakers to exceedingly high and exceedingly low points, often separated by just a year or two.

Proof positive that Nvidia was one heckuva buy at $21.35 in 2005—my original pick is now a 750-bagger. But it was also a heckuva buy at $50 (2009), and $307 (2017)—each time higher, but still a great pick (we'll cover this more in Chapter 2). And when you really think about it, it was a heckuva buy every *other* year in between. **And every single day of any of those years.**

Proof positive that if you want Nvidias in your future, the habit you need to start with is:

RULE NUMBER ONE:
...→ **LET YOUR WINNERS RUN. HIGH.** ←...

You don't *have* to follow this rule every time, or even at all. Some investors whom I know and respect never really do. (Most investors I do not respect never, ever do.)

But just realize if you *don't* make a habit of this rule, you'll never have the moon.

Oh, and one more thing. For storytelling purposes, I've used our original cost basis of $21.35 and traced Nvidia's rise to $16,115, multiplying over 750 times your money over nearly 20 years.[7] But as I mentioned with Starbucks earlier, most winning companies split their stocks, and Nvidia was no exception. Four times over the past 20 years, the company split its stock.[8] Shareholders today now have 120 shares for every one share they owned back in 2005, when I first recommended it.

Stock splits reduce the share price while increasing the number of shares *in equal proportion*—the pizza stays the same size, it just has more slices. So while Nvidia's share price *would* have climbed to $16,115 without splits, thanks to those splits, the stock now trades around $134. And our original cost basis? It's effectively been reduced to just 16 cents.[9]

For newcomers, rest assured: Nvidia was never a penny stock (don't buy penny stocks!). It's just that, for Rule Breaker investors like us,

---

7   As Nvidia paid some dividends, my adjusted buy price is now effectively $19.56, so as of the close of 2024 the pick all-in is up 823 times in value.

8   2-for-1 in 2006, 3-for-2 in 2007, 4-for-1 in 2021, and 10-for-1 in 2024.

9   16 cents! It's become a special number for me (cf. p. 62). (Technically, it's 16.17 cents.)

stock splits eventually give us incredibly low cost bases that have to be recalculated after years of holding.

It's a beautiful "problem" to have.

THE ROWBOAT SYNDROME

"The Rowboat Syndrome" is a lovely phrase that I borrow from Jack Bogle, one of many great lines and stories I've learned from the Vanguard founder, investing master, and great friend of The Fool. It's Jack's concept, but I'm going to put my own words (and spin) to it....

As we're paddling down the river of life as investors, which direction should we be looking?

Do you want to be in a rowboat? Most of the world is, because when you're in a rowboat, you're looking backward. So many market commentators, and indeed our fellow humans—we're not just talking about the stock market, here—are fixated on what has already happened. They're looking backward as they—*row, row, row*—move forward through time, down the river of life.

And here's what happens to the rowboaters, that *syndrome* part:

The market starts going up, but they haven't invested. Looking backward, they can so clearly see what has happened: Once again, the market is up—*row, row, row*—and *they missed it*. It's obvious now! And oh my golly... what?! The market just went up *another* year (not that surprising—the stock market rises on average two years out of every three). That first year up was "shame on you, stock market," but that second year up became "shame on me." The rowboaters had been waiting for a dip, a dip which never came, and so as they dip their oars in the river—*row, row, row*—they start thinking *they're* the dips. They should have been invested all along. And so, now with the benefit of hindsight (the only sight they're using), they finally decide they've made a huge mistake staying out of the market, and they finally—*row, row, row*—buy *in*....

And what do you think is about to happen?

Right... the market is probably about to drop. It's had a good couple of years! Valuations might be stretched, and there's likely some silliness in the system—companies of questionable merit driven by big-talking founders and promotional investor relations people are catching undeserved interest… and then the bear market sets in. Bear markets last 18 months on average, and they're never fun.

The stock market always goes down faster than it goes up, but it always goes up more than it goes down.

This line of thinking is unknown to rowboaters. They're now three full years down the river of life—*row, row, row*—out of the market the first two, and finally in, just in time to lose money. All they see (just behind them) is wreckage. They blame themselves (which in some ways they should), and now after "12 months of this mess," they rue the day they ever (finally) bought stocks, and *sell*.

And—*row, row, row*—what do you think is about to happen… next? Right.

It's brilliantly evocative of human psychology of which we all, in various contexts, have been guilty! It basically explains why many people *buy high* and *sell low*. And may well do it again. And again. That is the Rowboat Syndrome. (I hope I did it justice, Jack.)

Now I want to extend this metaphor in my own way, in support of Habit #1. Because to the rowboaters I say this:

"Toss away your rowboat and at least try a canoe!"

Because when you're in a canoe, you're facing forward. You recognize that what truly matters is what comes *next* around that bend in the river as you paddle forward—*paddle, paddle, paddle*—looking the right way. Here, you're not going to make the mistake of all those ~~pikers~~ rowboaters, obsessing over what's already happened and missing out on what's coming next. You can *see* what's ahead, you're paddling right toward it, eyes wide open, looking forward, not backward. This is definitely an improvement.

And yet! And yet… having spent my own time paddling through summer camps in the lakes of Maine, I know there's a better way. Because—*paddle, paddle, paddle*—you can't go very fast or very far in a canoe. Maybe you catch a current here and there, but much of the time, it becomes increasingly taxing. Each stroke demands another, and you need to stay alert to random obstacles like fallen branches or even snakes which, if you encounter them, you'd have to fend off with your paddle.

Canoes have their advantages over rowboats, but not that many, and—whoa!—you have to keep maintaining your balance to avoid tipping.

Which is why I want to take the analogy one step further by urging you to **toss away your paddle and kick that canoe aside, because there's a much more efficient way to navigate this breezy stream. And that's with a sailboat!**

The beauty of the stock market, as anyone who's studied it knows, is that it tends to rise 10% annualized over long periods of time. That's without you doing anything. The wind at your back is just going to blow. Doesn't it make sense to harness that power?

Those long-term market returns are the wind at your back. Thanks to deep-seated, logical, repeatable, though never entirely predictable dynamics, that wind (shifty as it sometimes is) will keep on blowing your whole life long—much more often at your back than in your face. The rowboaters don't get this; for them, the wind seems always in their face. The canoers don't get it either; for them, the wind doesn't matter much.

Ah, but you and I have chosen a sailboat. We're in it together, and you brought drinks! Jack Bogle's here, too, with all his Bogleheads and indexers! With the spinnaker set and that delightful breeze at our backs, what an awesome trip we get to enjoy as investors. We can sit back in the boat and let the wind push us forward, with compounding effects. All the way down that breezy river. Sure, bad weather will come, and occasionally we'll need to tack, but over the long run (and it's going to be a long run), we'll greatly enjoy the sights and camaraderie, and have fun getting rich together as the winds push us forward.

Sail on, silver girl.

BUT WHAT ABOUT WHEN BAD THINGS HAPPEN TO GOOD STOCKS?

Nvidia gives you a case study of what investing in a great stock truly looks and feels like. My rowboat-canoe-sailboat metaphor gives you a vivid illustration of what investing in the markets for a lifetime feels like. I hope these examples are helping you see your way to this #1 Habit!

When I think about all those paddlers in their canoes, as well as the people who owned Nvidia for just a year or two (whether up *or* down—they simply missed the "retire early" part), what we're really discussing is the opposite of Habit #1: *not* letting your winners run. And most of the time, that means you were trading.

Trading is the antithesis of investing.

Many people use the terms interchangeably. I do not. I see the difference in my own results and in those of fellow Fools who have been with me in the sailboat for years (or, at this point, decades). Investing may not beat trading every day of the week, but that's because only trading is itself trading every day of the week! Investing beats trading over the weeks, years, decades. Over the only term that matters: the long term.

But maybe these rose-tinted analogies I'm proffering are... irresponsibly carefree? I'm sure I must be giving the buy-and-hold crowd *way* too much of a pass. **Behavioral economics tells us that the pain of loss is three times the joy of gain.**[10] Stuff happens! Markets "crash." And traders are nimble, they watch their charts, they don't sit on losing positions. Hey, from 2005–2024, Nvidia sometimes went sideways for *years*. You could have traded in and out of that thing a bunch and made real money. Several times, too, the stock lost *50% or more*, over a gut-wrenching, face-melting year *or less*. Plus, not just Rule Breaker stocks but the whole market goes south regularly, and usually—at least once a decade—it goes to Antarctica!

Boats? Boats of every kind capsize! Trains? They can derail. Sluggers strike out. Even Babe Ruth....

HOME RUNS VS. STRIKEOUTS

Even people who neither follow sports nor live in the United States may still have some association with George Herman "Babe" Ruth. During

---

10 Daniel Kahneman and Amos Tversky formalized this observation as "prospect theory" in 1979, and "loss aversion" and related concepts are now widely recognized and cited.

his professional career from 1914 to 1935, Ruth hit more home runs than anyone up to that point in baseball history. In 1920, Babe Ruth alone hit more home runs (54) than *any other team* in the American League. His total home run record of 714 stood for decades, finally eclipsed by Hank Aaron in 1974. Along with his bat, Babe could also pitch, and on top of these things carried a larger-than-life personality which meant for decades, Babe reigned supreme. For now, he is the greatest baseball player of all time.[11]

But, while Ruth was phenomenally productive and successful as a hitter, he also racked up an all-time record for futility: Babe Ruth struck out 1,330 times.

One, two, three strikes you're out. Nobody knew that better than The Babe!

Picture Ruth, over and over again, more than a thousand times, sheepishly walking back to the dugout with that shame-faced grin, hearing some boos. I'm sure he got called a bum a lot.

Given that "the greatest hitter of all-time" struck out far more than he hit home runs, what are we to make of this? Is it admirable?

The answer lies in the impact of these respective actions. On average, *five runs win a Major League Baseball game.* A home run not only scores a run on its own, but can also drive in additional runs with players on base. So, one home run takes you 20%+ to winning. On the flip side, a strikeout generates one of the three outs a team is given for each of the nine innings in a game. Sure, strikeout... bummer! Yet, a strikeout takes you just 3.7% (1/27th) of the way to losing.

The comparison isn't even close: A single home run is *far* more impactful than a single strikeout. In fact, even if a player strikes out *four* times every single game—over and over, known as a "golden sombrero"— *but hits a home run on his fifth at-bat,* that player would be on the short list every year for league's Most Valuable Player.

---

11 And could be eclipsed: Today's phenomenon, Shohei Ohtani, is rewriting record books and astonishing fans (me included) with his extraordinary ability to both pitch and hit at an elite level, echoing The Babe in a way we haven't seen in nearly a century. That said, legends must be built up over time.

What's true in baseball is *truer* in investing, where the contrast is even sharper.

Consider the value of a baseball four-bagger (a home run) versus what Peter Lynch calls a four-bagger in investing. A baseball four-bagger scores one run (ka-*ching!*) and the hitter stops at home plate, no matter how far the ball travels. But in investing, a four-bagger—a stock that quadruples your money (*ka-ka-ka-CHING!*) can keep going. It can keep going a long, long time. We've already seen an iconic example of this, and there are plenty more to come.

WHY PEOPLE DON'T GET IT REASON #1: MATH

On December 11, 2018, The Motley Fool ran a simple poll on Twitter/X with just one question and two possible answers.

Which pairing of investment outcomes is more appealing to you:

- A 10-bagger and a 70% loser
- Two stocks each up 40%

(*What's your answer?*)

As of this writing, the poll has received 2,574 votes, and it's a dead heat. With all precincts reporting in, the first option (big winner and big loser) captured 50.2% of the tally, while the second option (two steady winners) secured 49.8%.

The comments below (which you can still view) include this response from my friend Hodges (@_Hdgs): "The results of this survey make me sad."

There are certainly arguments for preferring just steady-Eddie, disruption-free winners. It's also possible the poll's wording (which I didn't craft) may have confused the people of Twitter/X with the phrase "10-bagger." Had it said "900% winner and a 70% loser," the results could skew differently.

But as Aaron (@PegasusJockey) well conveys, "It's not that hard guys! You take two stocks and invest $2,000 in each one. Scenario number one you have $20,600. Scenario number two you have $5,600." Like comparing the value of home runs versus strikeouts... it's not even close.

WHY PEOPLE DON'T GET IT REASON #2: BIOLOGY

Give yourself a gold star if you easily saw through that last one.

I bet the majority of my readers are sporting a gold star about now, but don't let it go to your head. Because let's talk about that: What's in your head. Specifically, let's confront the mountain of studies[12] that generally points to the following truism (slipped into the middle of a paragraph a few pages back):

The pain of loss is three times the joy of gain.

This is critically important to understand. For reasons tied to our survival instincts,[13] humans are biologically hardwired toward what psychologists and behavioral economists call "loss avoidance." This traces back to our evolutionary roots, where losing access to food, shelter, or social standing could be life-threatening. Our brains are designed to protect us, making us more sensitive to the risks of *losing* something than to the potential benefits of gaining something equivalent. Our biological wiring favors caution and stability over the uncertain potential of rewards.

---

12   I'm a fan of the work of Barbara Fredrickson, the world's foremost expert on positive emotions who delivered this remarkable talk (tinyurl.com/4d6m859e); if you do take the time to watch it, appreciate how she actually invokes a sailboat metaphor of her own which jibes beautifully with ours. Also so helpful here is Shirzad Chamine (*Positive Intelligence*). Of course, there are lots of studies like this: tinyurl.com/yc89uy4k. Then there is the Nobel-Prize-winning behavioral economics work of Kahneman and Tversky, and others. Not everyone agrees on exactly three... I'm rounding a bit either way. The overall point is much more important than the coefficient's first decimal place....

13   In other words, that you're even here is because your ancient ancestors evolved this way... coded into their, and your, DNA.

Let's talk about it in an investing context. The most money you can lose on a bad stock pick (I've gotten close) is 100%. That's the worst you can do. Your biggest strikeouts.

What's the best you can do?

Hundreds of times your money. Nvidia is a prime example. We've already covered its extraordinary performance: a staggering 75,379%, or 750+ times our money. (And counting. We're still holding.)

So while the worst you can do is -100%, the best you can do is, quite literally, *infinite*.

The pain of loss for human nature being three times the joy of gain might serve us well in some contexts. But in the realm of investing, it's pure poison. It's the exact opposite of how you *should* think about your money, because:

The joy of investment gains is potentially *infinite* times the pain of loss.

Read that again. Keep reading until it sinks in. Make it a little affirmation you mouth quietly every time you touch your purse or wallet, until it's wired into your psyche, as it is in mine. Our knee-jerk human discomfort with loss may be much stronger than our joy from gain. But in Rule Breaker Investing, this flips. With your investment dollars, we're turning the innate ratios that govern most of our unwitting species (... especially those traders), upside-down.

This is also why I focus on learning bigger lessons—investing, business, and life lessons—from *success* rather than failure, and why I suggest you do the same. I transparently acknowledge my worst stock picks, then forget them and write them off. Your investment wins will leave your worst losses utterly in the dust, if you're playing the game right. So too I find that focusing on what's working, being positively intelligent and learning from success (mine or others'), has benefited me far more than dwelling on failures.

Now you know why most people don't get it. For some it might be math. For most, it's their own biology playing tricks on their psychology.

And with that, let's bring the single longest chapter of this book to a close, with one final section. *My favorite.*

LOSING TO WIN

You will lose, and you will lose *a lot* as a Rule Breaker investor.

Near the end of my stock picking for The Motley Fool, I dedicated an entire podcast to drive this point home, aptly titled "Losing to Win."[14] In that November 2020 podcast, I revealed that I had made exactly 389 consecutive monthly Rule Breakers service picks—two every month since October 2004—*and...*

(... please avert your gaze... *nothing to see here...* skip the bold and italics and just start again in a couple paragraphs, thank you very much?)...*fully 63 of those 389 stock picks had lost 50% or more.*

I hate that. It's painful. It's shameful. People followed—paid for—my advice. *I* followed my own advice. But I said then, and I'll tell you now: *You need to be prepared for this if you're going to be a Rule Breaker.* Because if you're not ready to lose, you're not truly a Rule Breaker. You have to be willing to lose.

Here's why: Because even though I had 63 *minus 50%+ losers* in the 389 picks I'd made over 16+ years (sixty-three!)...

... there's good news:

The 63rd best performer I picked, HubSpot, was up 402% at that point. That's not my best stock; it's not even in my top 50. But HubSpot, at number 63, had already made four times the money that any of my 63 biggest losers had lost. (As of this writing it's now up 904%.)

Are you doing the math with me (better than 49.2% of our Twitter/X poll respondents)?

If the worst you can do is lose 100%, and none of my 63 duds even reached that threshold... and if just my 63rd best pick was up 402%, you can see why, despite so many mind-numbingly bad stock picks, we had one of the great stock-market advisory services of all time.

And remember, that's just the 63rd best pick. The best performer in Rule Breakers at that point was Tesla, up 125 times in value since I'd first picked it (still holding!) using my Six Traits of a Rule Breaker Stock

---

14 It's been a few years since then, and so the numbers will have only become more pronounced! The underlying truth remains unchanged.

construct in November 2011. **Tesla's gains alone exceeded all of the losses from all those 63 minus 50%+'er stocks, combined.**

In fact, **the gains from that one Tesla stock pick were more than** *three* **times all those horrific losses, combined.**

The only way to uncover this was by following my Rule Breaker frameworks diligently, over a long period of time, and discovering the kind of gold that the Count of Monte Cristo once found in a cave—hard to find, mysterious, and immensely lucrative. Just to punch it home, the second-best performer for Rule Breakers then, **MercadoLibre**, had increased 103 times in value. And there were 60 others in between HubSpot (+401.8%) and Tesla and MercadoLibre, all having risen from 5 to 100 times in value.

It's also worth highlighting for any skeptics that Motley Fool Stock Advisor, which I also helped oversee, ran back even further (March 2002) and had even better performers (we'll discuss some later). The key point: It exhibited the *exact same dynamic*—embarrassingly bad losers that, if combined into a group, were completely overshadowed by the profits from just the service's best winner (then Netflix, now Nvidia).

When you find Rule Breaker stocks, *AND* develop Habit #1, giving them time... *this will be what happens.*

Say it again with me! Sing it: With Rule Breaker Investing, **the value of winning completely wipes out the cost of losing**.

Yet most people lack a real education in investing, feel overwhelmed by macroeconomics headlines or TV talking heads self-servingly telling them "Buy and Hold is Fatal." These poor unfortunate souls (a.k.a. nearly everyone) are gripped by a fear of losing driven by their natural psychology, and end up rowing down the river of time in boats facing backward, causing them to trade too much.

Meanwhile, the math of investing beautifully confounds the psychology we're all born with. The promise is immense: As winners win, their gains far outweigh the losers that lose. But unless you're visionary enough to recognize this, and daring enough to act on your convictions, you'll miss out on the prosperity that the market has been lavishing on our society decade after decade, despite all the bear markets and crashes: *Huge* gains.

Can you see the truth?

Can you translate that understanding into action (or inaction)?

Can you form **a new Habit**, refining your approach—not necessarily with all your money all at once (though all mine is fully invested this way)—but maybe by starting *now*, with just a portion?

Can you be not only okay with, but genuinely excited about, *Losing to Win?*

If you can say "Yes" to at least a couple of the questions above, then I believe you're already on track to start stretching this new muscle, cultivating this *new* habit... and there's *new music* playing in your future!

Nvidia is just one stock, one of many examples. But that new music sounds like Nvidia, which, as I said at the start, "tells you all you need to know, if you will but listen."

···→ **RULE NUMBER ONE:**
LET YOUR WINNERS RUN. HIGH. ←···

CHAPTER 2

ADD UP, *DON'T* DOUBLE DOWN

O N THE FACE of it, Habit #2 is not too complicated. The complication may just be in the doing.

··→ ADD UP, DON'T DOUBLE DOWN. ←··

By "add," I mean adding new money into investments you already hold.

Having new money is a good problem to have! I hope you'll have that problem every two weeks with your next paycheck, and that you'll pay yourself first by automatically deducting a portion of each paycheck (so you don't see that money hit your checking account), and overall saving at least 5% of your salary (we Fools aim for 10%+). Over your life, make this problem *increasingly problematic* (+$$$!) by growing your value and becoming increasingly important to your organization and the world.

Once you have made this a big and growing problem, the first solution is to invest new money into new investments, or existing investments that you already have.

We're not building a portfolio right now, that's for Part III. For now, we'll focus on adding money to existing investments where we *add up*, not double down. Okay?

Okay... but why?

"BUY LOW, SELL HIGH"

You're reading the *Rule Breaker* book, so you should expect my approach to run counter to human psychology, expectations, and old wisdoms, specifically the threadbare phrase: *Buy low, sell high*. These are **four of the most harmful words** ever strung together (by traders?) to fool[15] the unwitting public. They are trotted out as the brainlessly "obvious" advice, the punchline to the question, "How do you get rich in the stock market?"

The problem is that right after buying (buying high not low, more in Chapter 9), the very *next* word is: Sell. Some people are urged to buy only if they know their target price to sell. This proves they have a sell discipline, which is deemed obligatory if you want to call yourself an investor. *"Ah, but what is your **sell discipline**?"* the serious professionals (investors and journalists) ask, staring down their pince-nez at you.

I won't repeat Chapter 1's points, but you already know to let your winners run, which talk of sell discipline—and buy low, *sell* high—subverts.

The phrase I suggest you memorize (and stick on your fridge) is: **Buy high and try not to sell**. With Rule Breaker Investing, we focus on stocks that go lower-left to upper-right over time. When adding new money, invest in these rising stocks. The ones going up.

Most people do the opposite, buying low and adding to losing positions. They *average down*, putting new money toward their underperformers to bring those losing investments back into parity with the other (winning) stocks in the portfolio. Diversified mutual funds do this, en masse.

This phenomenon, explained to me by my father Paul Gardner Jr. at an impressionable age (thanks, Dad), is throwing good money after bad. This tendency causes funds and people to underperform the market averages over time. It reflects the human urge to get back to even, otherwise known as the sunk cost fallacy.

---

15 From day one, I've drawn the *critical* distinction between "Fools" and "fools." I celebrate Foolishness and try to be a (capital F) Fool—like the court jesters and different-thinkers (Steve Jobs: "Think different") of yore. The opposite, the common fool, a.k.a. nitwits, idiots, imbeciles, the like, are the fools you hear about the other 98% of the time. That's the traditional kind that no one aspires to: small f.

Framing our failing investments as a Quest to Get Back to Even is misguided. Many investors view it this way, and I've spoken with them at conferences, book signings, and online for years. I challenge their conventional wisdom.

Don't try to get back to even.

Reassess every investment by focusing not on where it's been, but where it's going. Whether a stock is up 80% or down 80%, it's your capital at stake, and your goal is to optimize the returns. Don't fixate on the entry price or obsess over getting back to even. Instead, ask your new savings, "New savings, how can I invest you as well as I possibly can, going forward?"

Past gains and losses are irrelevant to this question. The market doesn't care what you paid. There is no ceiling for your gains, and no reason that your 80% losses should ever get back to even. People live so in fear of an 80% loss that they'll hold their money in that stock, possibly for years, when they could have cut bait and followed their nose to where the real success would come next.

This is not the successful psychology you want to impose on your fresh crop of new savings.

When a stock of mine struggles, I prefer to let it recover on its own. "You got yourself into this mess!" I fume, the scolding parent. "Now get yourself out of it." This is especially true of the breed of stocks shared with you throughout this book, the Rule Breakers. They are not the unsinkable Molly Browns of the investing world. When something goes wrong with upstart innovators like Peloton or GoPro, these companies can plummet and never come back. This is the nature of Rule Breaker Investing. Part of me certainly admires "too big to fail" companies like Walmart, Boeing, and Microsoft, each with long stretches of serious underperformance and critical problems that nevertheless bounced back over time. FitBit, Rosetta Stone, Blue Apron, TiVo… not so much.

Thus, it's as simple as adding to your winning positions and ignoring your losers until they get themselves out of the mess they've made, which for me means **rising to the point they're up, not down**, where they've made, not lost, money for your portfolio. The one mistake I have never made and will never make, that has ruined some, is throwing good money after bad. We're never trying to get back to even. That way madness, a.k.a. extreme poverty, lies.

That's why the vital practice of Habit #2 is such a friend:

···→ ADD UP, DON'T DOUBLE DOWN. ←···

Make it an option *only* to add to your winners, to what's doing well in this world, never the opposite. Do so with the knowledge that most others (including most professionals, and almost all large mutual funds as a requirement to maintain diversity) are doing the opposite: rebalancing, averaging down, cutting the flowers and watering the weeds, as the old saw goes. By watering your flowers instead you are nurturing growth. More power to you and to those dollars you're adding!

Here's Habit #2 put another way: ***Throw good money after good!***

OPPORTUNITIES > "BARGAINS"

"Language is the dress of a thought," said Samuel Johnson. I loved majoring in English literature and it's lines like these that have stayed with me and continue to add value. The quality of our thinking is often linked to the language we use. And vice versa, the quality of our language often influences the quality of our thinking. Scrutinize your own diction, as well as the word choice of others. Language matters. It's worth more than its weight in gold. (Especially in light of its being abstract and weightless.)

The word "bargain" is a good example. Many investors love it; it speaks to them like a retailer's "30% OFF!" sign. They're ever preparing for when stocks are on sale. If you liked it at $100, the thinking goes, you're going to love it at $52. And sometimes, they're right. Bargain-hunter nirvana.

But bargains of this kind don't come along frequently. Meanwhile, the market rises day by day, two years out of every three, and over almost every decade. Many great Rule Breaker stocks show up as early-stage companies, *never* priced as bargains, offering us the great opportunities of our investing lifetimes.

This is why I favor the word "opportunity." **I don't seek bargains; I**

seek opportunities. For market-whacking returns, opportunities have always served me better. If you start saying, and seeking, "opportunities," you're much more likely to find them. Adopting this mindset will serve you well when investing new money into existing investments. Habit #2 is to pursue opportunities, not bargains.

I hope the point is clear. It's one thing to understand it, and another to feel it and *act on it*. So, here's one more reflection to help you over the hump....

DIPS WAIT FOR DIPS

Do you wait to buy on dips? Many investors do. I don't.

For starters, some stocks never really dip. Or at least not for long. If you follow the logic, you'll see that these are often the best performers (because after all, they never dipped, right?). Which means that if you're sitting back waiting for The Dip, you'll miss The Sizzle. I prefer sizzle to dip.

Those who inveterately wait to buy on dips very likely miss or badly have to chase the best-performing stocks of this or any era. A standout Motley Fool Rule Breakers stock since the mid-2000s has been Chipotle, a January 17, 2007 recommendation by my brilliant colleague Rick Munarriz (we're still holding). Rick picked Chipotle at the memorable cost basis of $1.212.[16]

Those who held off buying this stock, waiting for the dip, got one opportunity six months later in mid-July. The stock, now "on sale," had downdrafted 11% from $1.80 to $1.60. It was just for two weeks; you'd have had to time that precisely. And maybe a few did, picking it up at $1.60 on the dip.

However, remember that our cost basis was $1.212, meaning the dips who bought on the dip paid 33% more than those who bought the sizzle.

By contrast, the three worst selections my colleagues and I made that year—Syneron Medical (ELOS), Force Protection (FRPT), and

---

16   Well, it used to be more memorable. Rick actually picked it at the seeing double-double cost basis of $60.60. But after not once splitting its stock in its 30-year history, in June 2024 Chipotle finally executed a 50-for-1 stock split (the largest ever on the New York Stock Exchange).

Jones Soda (JSDA)—offered *numerous* dips on their way to 30% to 40% declines in 2007. Thus, the dippy investor waiting for dips could have *easily* bought these three worst-performing stocks. (These awful stock picks in a horrendous market environment, two by yours truly, ended up with final returns of −77%, −92%, and −82% respectively.) This is how people start out picking stocks, miss winners, buy losers, lose money, and are then out of the game. "Stock picking is not for me," they say... waiting for dips. This book aims to correct that!

As we near an end, I hasten to add two things. First, my Losing to Win cardinal theme shared in the last chapter is evident here once again. You probably think—I kind of do, too!—that picking four stocks in 2007, with three of them down between −77% and −92%, is absolutely abysmal.

But the fourth was Chipotle, which has risen for us 4,875% to date.

Many will live in fear of a single loss of −75%, let alone three stocks picked in the same year *worse* than that. But losses of −77%, −82%, and −92% melt away when averaged into the four-digit blowout gain of +4,875%.

If winning big over the long term involves suffering horrible-looking two-digit percentage drops—and I think it does—we'll invite them every day of the week and twice on Sundays. Because again, it's about the sizzle, not the dip.[17]

When you...

⋯⟶ ADD UP, DON'T DOUBLE DOWN. ⟵⋯

... you are making a commitment to the *companies* you want to own, not the stocks you're going to buy on dips. Be an investor, not a share-price guesser. To own and keep adding to the market's best stocks, this is the surest way. You'll end up a winning Chipotle investor, instead of just a dippy Chipotle watcher. Hold the *queso*!

---

17 Rule Breakers picked two stocks a month, so I'm just featuring the three biggest 2007 losers and the biggest winner. It's worth noting there were six other winners picked that ill-fated year that the service still holds with gains of 100%–1,400%. But if I put that above in the text, it would just look like bragging. So I put it in the footnote.

CHAPTER 3

INVEST.
FOR AT LEAST
THREE YEARS.

"YOU STILL LIKE cloud computing stocks," the host queried me during the commercial break, "after *yesterday*?"

I was co-hosting the early morning CNBC market show with a smart young anchor. Our perspectives couldn't have been further apart. During the first commercial break, I'd mentioned several of my favorite stocks, like *Salesforce*... and her jaw dropped. The cloud computing sector had sold off 7%–10% the day before.

"You still like cloud computing stocks... after *yesterday*?!"

My co-host (we shall call her "After Yesterday") wasn't a day trader or a high-frequency-trading supercomputer. This was a well-educated, successful broadcast journalist who got up at dawn to cover the markets. People tuned in to her to learn the day's ins and outs of business and market developments.

Except maybe in a sense she was a day trader. Anyone who follows the markets for a living and makes other people feel like rubes for still liking a stock "after yesterday?!" would seem to be day trading the headlines, trends, and buzz, even if not day trading the stock market.

If you follow something minute by minute, every zig, zag, pass, shot, or tackle becomes noteworthy. You magnify it. And heck, After Yesterday isn't being paid for her financial advice. She's great at what she does; anchoring live TV at any hour of the day is a demanding job. Just don't confuse her perspective with financial expertise or let it guide your money.[18]

In most aspects of life, I'd bet After Yesterday is well-mannered and exemplary. It's only with the stock market that she thinks and likely acts contrary to her and your best outcomes. Ironic, and kinda crazy.

If you ever wonder how common Fools like you and me can outperform Wall Street and its indices, you now know your answer. The surest way to beat the market over time involves maintaining the same equanimity and perspective with your money that you do in other aspects of your life. Maybe Billy Joel crooned the greatest investment secret of all: "Don't go changin." In other words, buy stocks to keep them, not trade them! You'll do so much better if you:

⋯→ INVEST. FOR AT LEAST THREE YEARS. ←⋯

If your absolute minimum holding period is less than three years, you're doing it wrong.

INVESTIRE: PUTTING ON THE JERSEY

We often misunderstand what "invest" means and what "investing" looks like.

The Latin root for "invest" is *investire*, meaning "to put on the clothes, wear the garments." Think of a related phrase like "priestly vestments."

Picture fans wearing the jerseys of their favorite teams. As they walk to the stadium, find the way to their seats, cheer their team on, they are sporting the home team colors. And whether their team wins or loses, they keep that jersey on. Whether their team has a good or bad season, they keep that jersey on.

Why?

Because they're deeply *invested*. (Ironically, many may be more invested in their sports teams than in something of far more value, the

---

18 I'd guess some people watching CNBC think the opposite.

financial investments they make.) Sports fans know their team is not going to win every game or year. Rule Breaker investors know the same of our stocks. If you find a great team, stick with it.

"Putting on the clothes" can be literal. People wear shirts with an Apple logo, love their Lululemons, have "Harley" tattooed on their shoulder.[19] You likely have logoed garments in your wardrobe. So my wishes for you are (a) that you own those stocks, and (b) that those investments will outlast your clothes.

Whether or not you have the shirt yet, I want you to love the companies you're invested in. My portfolio includes enterprises that I believe do good things in this world, are purpose-driven, manage for the long term, show resilience, exhibit optionality. I believe their success leads to a better world. When you're actually *invested* like this, **it's natural even in hard times to keep that jersey on**.

If people treated financial investments like their lifelong emotional investments in their sports teams, they'd be smarter, happier, and richer. Some trading may make sense for some people, but the standard presentation of market news coverage akin to a daily race program, inducing the audience to trade rather than invest, is tragic. It's hard to quantify the resulting human misery.

Investing, not trading, should be the default.

I'm not here to denigrate trading *per se*, particularly as done by professionals like bond traders or futures traders who enable and support markets. We do need traders for market activity and liquidity, which allows equity investors today to enter and exit positions in one second— about 4,233,600 times faster than buying or selling a house.[20]

That said, most market crashes and frauds stem from traders racing against time to transact, *unloading* their holdings—quick!—before the world discovers their fleeting value.

For you and me, there are many more interesting ways to spend one's brief time on this earth than staring at wiggles on charts, sharing morning

---

19 These are not the same people.

20 60 seconds in a minute × 60 minutes in an hour × 24 hours in a day × 49 days needed to sell a house on average.

coffees with After Yesterday, or habitually following the markets, crypto, or forex all day. Too many more urgent needs, too many more interesting things in life. Good non-professional traders are rare indeed, but even if you're one such, trading consumes so much time.... Good news! If you trade these habits for Habit #3, **you enjoy life more and do better with your investments.**

My favorite tradeoffs are *when there's no tradeoff.*

Imagine starting out as a fan of your hometown team, and then a wise figure—your grandmother or uncle—sits you down sternly but lovingly, and says, "Now that you're becoming a fan, I really hope you'll think seriously about cheering for this team *for at least three years*." Ridiculous, right? It's your hometown team (or favorite brand, or movement, or idea, or person). Having to impose a three-year minimum commitment seems ludicrous.

Seems just as ludicrous to me to have to say (but I say it!), develop habit #3:

⋯→ INVEST. FOR AT LEAST THREE YEARS. ←⋯

THE DEAD-ARM INITIATIVE

Much of the juice in these pages comes from my exemplars: my dad, Peter Lynch, Warren Buffett, Kermit the Frog, the ancient Greeks. But here's something truly original: Let me be the first financial author to invite you to give me a dead-arm.[21]

That's right: Anytime we meet and you ever hear me say the phrase "long-term investor" (I'll even throw in "long-term investing," too), you may give me a dead-arm. Walk up, make a fist, lead with your knuckles, and rap me just above my bicep. For a few seconds, you'll make my arm

---

21   Under very specific circumstances! (Please keep reading.)

feel numb, weak, unresponsive... but I'll understand. *You just reminded me not to say "long-term investor."* It's my Dead-Arm Initiative.

Why? *To honor and protect the word "investing."* We've covered its etymology. You know its antithesis. Thus, you now know an eternal truth that most people don't: **Investing is inherently long term**. So when someone says that three-word phrase, they're guilty of tautology. (It also misleads, suggesting *other* forms of investing besides the long term. There are not. "Short-term investing" is an oxymoron.)

I once got this podcast question: "Is short-term trading to fund long-term investing a good strategy?"

My 11th-grade composition teacher Mr. Kerrick would cross out a few words, making it simpler: "Is trading to fund investing a good strategy?"

Or, to paraphrase: "Is doing something bad, to achieve something good, a good strategy?!" No Machiavellian myself, you can imagine my answer.

Another podcast listener once threw me what I take as a high, high compliment, and he did it in so few words.[22] "From you, I learned the difference between trading and investing." I hope this book does the same for you....

Some years ago, we had a young employee named Mark Reagan at the Fool. He'd been raised right. His wonderful mother had said to him: "Mark, there are three ways to make money: with your brains, with your brawn, or with your money. Which will you choose?" Mark was fascinated by the third answer, "Make money with my money." What a world we were born into, where you can make money with your money!

But one thing is more precious: Our time. **Here's my definition of trading: *Spending lots of time trying to make money maybe half the time***. I don't think trading was on Mark's mom's list.

Even average investors outperform very good traders, with way less effort. Full stop. Brokerage firms find their passive accounts outperform their active ones.

Investors use time as our friend, not an enemy. Investors are far more tax-efficient. Investors have so many advantages! It amazes me how many

---

22 Thank you, Art Burke.

people think it's *impossible* to hold stocks. As if it takes some kind of great effort. Actually, it doesn't take any effort at all. It takes effort to sell (and then to re-buy, if people ever do).

It's called *investing*.

Which is why we don't need that beautiful word overloaded with unnecessary adjectives.

No one has yet given me a dead-arm. Sure, there's a chance this Fool will stumble, but I'm not trying to keep the fun all to myself. Help out your family and friends! Join the revolution: Start your own dead-arm initiative.

THE MARKET'S ROLLERCOASTER RIDE

The key with Habit #3, in addition to making it a habit, is to specify a minimum amount of time that forces you to recognize you're playing the long game. Three years is my bare minimum, but I prefer three decades.

Setting this minimum ties into the classic statistic that **the market drops one year in every three**. Recognizing this puts your mind in a place not governed by fear. You already know it: The market's fantastic decades-long rollercoaster ride will naturally include some stomach-flipping drops. Habit #3 steels your resolve not to let these drops prevent you from reaching your amazing destination.

And it is a fantastic rollercoaster ride, with *one big difference* between your investing and an actual rollercoaster. To demonstrate this, let's take a quick ride together on an amusement park rollercoaster, shall we...? Drop off your stuff in a nearby cubby.

Welcome! Please step into the rollercoaster car, strap in, and let's ensure the safety harness is secure. Get ready for fun: You're not *supposed* to lift your feet off the ground or put your hands in the air, but you can if you want to. Granted, spot internet research suggests half of all people do *not* enjoy rollercoasters. But it's only three minutes, and you did wait in line for 30 minutes for this. So!

Up-up-*up*-up we go... grinding... slowly... and then WHOOOOOOOOOOOOOOOOOOOSH!!!!! Down *really* fast! (Like the stock market, at times.) And then, you crank right around a loop! And then left—slam!—the other way, around a second loop...! And then: Up, up, grinding... slowly again... and then WHOOOOOOOSH! Another drop that—oh my golly—sends us up into a *loop-the-loop*?!

And the rest of it is similarly anxiety-filled and exhilarating at points, and there are a few rests baked in, and now here we come slowing down, to the finish line... all together now.... (Some might call that "retirement," might say that's *why* we took this ride in the first place.) And yet...

Shocker!

It all felt like a crazy rollercoaster ride. Like you remember, when you were a kid.

But the whole time, even though often you couldn't tell or feel it, with every passing loop, loop-the-loop, slow-roll up, and nauseating drop down, **the investing rollercoaster was taking you *higher and higher*.**

It didn't feel great having to sit through every drop. Especially since you couldn't get off (and might not have noticed all the 10% rises you were compounding).

Here's that one big difference I mentioned:

Unlike traditional rollercoasters, you didn't end where you started.

Unfasten that shoulder strap, push up the safety bar, and gather your belongings. And take a look: Because as it turns out, the *investing* rollercoaster took you up to the top of a *mountain*. And wow, look at that view.

The view from the end of the ride—worth every twist and dip. [Kauai]

···→ INVEST. FOR AT LEAST THREE YEARS. ←···

If they ever build an amusement park about stock picking, I hope the designers include this ride, the one you just rode: The Rule Breaker Rollercoaster.

Early on, you and your family would blow past a sign reading: "AFTER *YESTERDAY*?"

It would be the only rollercoaster in the world that doesn't deposit you where you started, but instead takes you far higher than you ever dreamed.

CHAPTER 4

FOLLOW THE FOUR TENETS OF CONSCIOUS CAPITALISM

WENDY KOPP FOUNDED Teach for America. In a 2022 address to Princeton graduates, speaking as a Princetonian herself to the most intelligent and sensitive generation ever yet born, she said of life's purpose (bold mine):

> In this era there's more attention than ever, especially among your generation, on personal well-being and finding 'balance.' What I've seen is that **the highest form of well-being is the exhilaration that comes from immersing ourselves in things that matter.** The path to happiness is not balance *per se*, but rather congruence between the values we hold most dear and where we spend our energy.

Kopp's exhortation to immerse ourselves in things that matter resonates deeply with me. Her prescription of purpose aligns with *Conscious Capitalism*, the groundbreaking book by John Mackey, the co-founder of Whole Foods, and academic Raj Sisodia. Conscious capitalism is vital for CEOs, MBA students, and our environment—but also crucial to your investing success. So, Habit #4 is simply:

→ **FOLLOW THE FOUR TENETS OF CONSCIOUS CAPITALISM.** ←

If you can't already recite them by heart, you will by the end of this chapter. I hope you'll remember, insist on, promote, and practice them for life.

#1 PURPOSE OVER PROFIT: THE SNAP TEST

Those young Princetonians and all their peers have been called the most purpose-seeking generation in history. Roy Spence, chairman of the Austin, TX-based brand-building firm GSD&M, may be the most quotable conscious capitalist of his generation. On my podcast he said:

> They're going to work for organizations and companies that have a purpose beyond making money. They're going to buy products and services from companies that treat their employees right, that treat the community right, that treat their country right, that treat the environment right. They're going to be looking for purpose-inspired organizations.
>
> So investors, before you put a dime in somebody's company, I would go ask the CEO, 'What is the purpose of your company?' Rather than have to pull out their business card because on the back it says, 'Blah, blah, blah, blah...' they ought to be able to say right off, 'Our purpose is to help people love where they live.' (By the way, that's Lowe's Companies: 'We help people love where they live.')
>
> So that would be the No. 1 question for my investment in the future.

In the same way that the "top dog and first-mover in an important, emerging industry" is the first trait I look for in Rule Breaker stocks (Chapter 7), purpose is the first tenet to spy out when extending your conscious capitalism telescope.

Of course we want our companies ultimately to show profit, great profit, but the ironic truth is that the ones that do, from one industry to the next, are often the companies that *uphold their purpose over their profits*.

The textbook examples are true: Under no regulatory thumb Johnson & Johnson did pull 31 million bottles of Tylenol during the 1982 poisoning scare; Patagonia does donate 1% of its *revenues* to the preservation and restoration of the natural environment; Ben & Jerry's does integrate social activism into its ice cream flavors and business model; Whole Foods has been rightly renowned for investing at great expense in sustainable agriculture; and Tesla's purpose statement isn't "to make a lot of money" or "put legacy automakers out of business," but, "To accelerate the world's transition to sustainable energy."

These companies and their ilk aren't just profitable; in some cases, they have the most (sometimes, all) of the profits in their industries. And it's because they are **powered by purpose**.

Powered by purpose works for profit, and not for profit. The best not-for-profits often do this very well. Internally and externally they exude their authentic purpose. Amnesty International, Doctors Without Borders, Habitat for Humanity, The Nature Conservancy, and The World Wildlife Fund all have (check it!) beautiful purpose statements that arouse our admiration, but only because they walk their talk. So do the best for-profit companies, and those are the ones I want you to make a *habit* of finding, following, and (if they check out) funding.

In *Rule Breakers, Rule Makers*, which I co-wrote with my brother Tom in 1999, I first explained "The Snap Test." The Snap Test (snap!) has stood the test of time and still helps me and others discern the power of purpose.

Imagine what the world would be like if, overnight, you snapped your fingers (snap!) and caused a company you're researching... to disappear!

Snap!

{*Poof.*}

Would anyone notice? Would anyone care?

Employees would notice, of course (if they hadn't also disappeared), but would consumers miss it? Would the business headlines (maybe national) lead with it? Would no other company be able to fill the gap? How many would notice and how many would care?

One of my favorite Shakespearean quotes applied to investing comes from *Henry IV, Part 1*. The proud Welsh character Glendower delivers this immortal line—at least it's immortal for me: "I say the earth did shake when I was born." Never mind that we now know thanks to sensitive seismographic equipment that the earth constantly shakes; when truly great companies are born, it shakes a little more! And that's where I want to put my money, in those companies that shake the earth when they're born.

So get in the habit of snapping your fingers when you build your watchlist of stocks. Adopt Habit #4 by looking at the purposes of companies. Amazon.com's purpose from its earliest days: "To be Earth's most customer-centric company." That made a big impression on me when I first picked the stock at a split-adjusted price of 16 cents on September 8, 1997. (Still holding.)

This makes even more sense in light of Habit #3, since we're going to be leaving our hard-earned money in our investments for years. Given that, we should insist that our companies do something important, something that matters in the world for good, that people notice and are grateful for.

Puts me in mind of this fabulous quotation from 19th-century American evangelist D.L. Moody: **"Our greatest fear should not be of failure, but of succeeding at something that doesn't really matter."** Similarly, I encourage you to fear your own portfolio if it's full of companies that don't really matter.

As a lifetime stockpicker, I do better when I listen for that snap, when I respect what the test teaches us. In short, buy companies that if they disappeared overnight, tons of people would notice and many would care. Those are the stocks that will do best in our portfolios over long periods.

I had no idea when I first wrote up the snap test that, in 2018, Disney would release *Avengers: Infinity War* with a "real world"[23] snap that seared this concept into our collective memory. The villain Thanos, having (spoiler alert!) obtained the six Infinity Stones, snaps his fingers at the movie's cliffhanger conclusion and disintegrates half of all life in

---

23   For those who, and they're out there, consider the Marvel Cinematic Universe real.

the universe. Ironically, I had picked Marvel stock for Motley Fool Stock Advisor partly using the snap test! That was June 7, 2002. More happy irony: Disney *snapped* up Marvel seven years later, making my $1.78 split-adjusted cost for Disney stock a huge winner. (Still holding.)

So when Thanos snapped for the whole world to see, he echoed something I'd conveyed 20 years earlier... which led many investors to the stock that spawned him.

Oh snap!

#2 WIN-WIN-WIN

Life, investing, and business aren't zero-sum games. Many see them this way, to their detriment.

Zero-sum, tradeoff-mentality thinkers use phrases like "dog-eat-dog" to describe their perception of this world, where one person's fortune implies someone else got bankrupted. In sports, sure, most of the time we play to final scores that determine winners and losers. But applying this view to reality is harmful.

Dogs, by the way, don't eat dogs. Dogs, by nature, are social animals that exhibit pack behavior. Cooperation and social bonds are essential for survival. While dogs may show aggression in disputes over territory, food, or social rank, the idea of dogs eating each other misrepresents their natural behavior. The same misrepresentation occurs in viewing life and business as zero-sum.

While I'd like to delve deeper into this point, we'll keep things high-level for *Rule Breaker Investing*. Humans, like dogs, are social animals. We thrive on cooperation, social hierarchy, and bonds essential for survival. Contrary to the dog-eat-dog view, business is more cooperative than competitive. Competition needs to exist (a huge strength of the system). But companies design, develop, and deploy their products and services using an amazing amount of collaboration globally to get you that avocado on your dish at the restaurant.[24]

To start with, employees collaborate with management and at the best companies mutual support, not animosity, defines the relationship. They cooperate, which means they outdo their competitors who fail to cooperate! And then there are natural business partners who work together, often across borders, to combine dozens if not thousands of components in your brand new smartphone. Many companies even partner with competitors (sharing technology and co-developing products) to combine industry-wide and global wins. The interdependence within the capitalist system, including between major competitors like the United States and China, is profound.

The best leaders at every level of our society operate with this win-win-win mentality. I win, you win, *they* win too. "They" might be the environment (thanks to Patagonia), or local communities (highlighted by Starbucks' community service and Fair Trade sourcing), or future generations (underscored by Tesla's commitment to sustainable energy).

Win-win-win has been described as the only truly ethical framework, and I have seen it first hand, starting with my friend John Mackey, the founder of Whole Foods, who published his life story, *The Whole Story*, in 2024. Before that, John co-wrote *Conscious Capitalism*, inspiring this chapter and Habit #4, wherein he wrote: "Purposeful companies ask questions such as these: Why does our business exist? Why does it need to exist? What core values animate the enterprise and unite all of our stakeholders?"

---

24 Another classic statement of this was made by Walter Lippmann in *The Good Society*: "The thinker, as he sits in his study drawing his plans for the direction of society, will do no thinking if his breakfast has not been produced for him by a social process which is beyond his detailed comprehension. He knows that his breakfast depends upon workers on the coffee plantations of Brazil, the citrus groves of Florida, the sugar fields of Cuba, the wheat farms of the Dakotas, the dairies of New York; that it has been assembled by ships, railroads, and trucks, has been cooked with coal from Pennsylvania in utensils made of aluminum, china, steel, and glass. But the intricacy of one breakfast, if every process that brought it to the table had deliberately to be planned, would be beyond the understanding of any mind. Only because he can count upon an infinitely complex system of working routines can a man eat his breakfast and then think about a new social order."

So, how do we spot companies with the win-win-win mentality? Look beyond just the balance sheet and the bottom line. Pay attention to leadership statements about purpose and core values—these often reflect a company's broader commitment to stakeholders. But it goes further. Actions speak louder than words. Seek out companies actively engaging in socially responsible initiatives, sustainable practices, or meaningful partnerships with their communities or the environment. Look for companies that are not only industry leaders but also innovators in how they treat employees, suppliers, and the world around them.

On my Rule Breaker Investing podcast, from 2015–2021 I picked 30 different baskets of five stocks each, called my five-stock samplers. These samplers highlighted various themes, and we would track their returns for three years to listen and learn. The 150 stocks as an overall basket gained 76%, vs. the S&P 500's gain of 40%, which made a pretty great (free) show for people skeptical that you can beat the market over volume and time.

One of my favorite of those five-stock samplers speaks to this chapter. Entitled "5 Stocks That Will Let You Eat Cake," selected in November 2017, it addressed the dog-eat-dog, zero-sum mentality by asserting you don't have to choose either/or. Instead, we can live and invest in a *both/and* world. This sampler showcases an abundance mentality, demonstrating that "we can have our cake and eat it too," defying those possessed of a tradeoff mentality. On that podcast, I introduced the first stock this way:

> I'm going to give you a choice here. You can either have the No. 1 company globally in e-commerce, or you can have the No. 1 leader in cloud-computing storage today. Which one would you take?

The (trick) answer was, of course, *both*. (For all five stocks.) The stock pick was Amazon.com, re-recommended 20 years after I first picked it (illustrating Habit #2!). Not all five stocks beat the stock market, but together they rose 115% over the following three years, obliterating the S&P 500's 39%. (Today, the basket is way higher.)[25]

---

25   Oh, and the other four: CBOE Global Markets, Match Group, Nvidia, and 2U.

"What do winners do?" the old saying goes, oft-repeated by me, particularly on my podcast. I know you know the punchline: "They win!" Winners win.

But real winners *win-win-win*, win for everyone.

#3 & #4 CONSCIOUS LEADERSHIP AND CONSCIOUS CULTURE

I've spent most of my ink this chapter on Purpose (tenet #1) and win-win-win (also termed "stakeholder orientation," tenet #2), as they are the more interesting dynamics to follow, embody, and make a habit of as an investor and leader.

The other two tenets of Conscious Capitalism are open-and-shut cases; they don't need extensive elaboration. They are conscious leadership and conscious culture.[26]

Conscious leadership is synonymous with servant leadership. Servant leaders don't reserve personal privileges for themselves. They frame their life's work as serving others (customers and employees), serving the higher purpose of their organization. These are the best leaders, not just in business, but in the entire world. I have met many of them personally, and can find more outstanding leaders in business than in politics or any other sphere of society.

Conscious culture describes the rich culture of companies regularly making "Best Companies to Work For" lists. The truly great companies—that will become the best long-term stocks—are those that engage not just the effort but the *hearts* of their employees. This is in part what makes them great, and so very hard to compete with!

Every customer wants to pay less, every employee wants to be paid more, every partner or supplier wants to be facing out your shop window, and

---

26 I totally encourage you to read about them: www.consciouscapitalism.org

every shareholder wants you to double their stock tomorrow. These incentives and instincts are all at odds with each other, and every business leader knows it.

Along with Wendy Kopp, who led off this chapter telling her fellow Princetonians that "balance" isn't the answer, I say the best leaders will not trade off, but will find solutions that win across *all* these dynamics. It's not always easy, but it's possible, and it's done by those wearing win-win-win-colored lenses all the time. You want to make a habit of finding, following, and funding them.

My aim is to make every chapter in this book a rich lesson on its own, so that anyone browsing one chapter and skipping the rest will still be left smarter, happier, and richer. So if this is the only chapter you browse and Habit #4 is all you glean, I am still smiling!

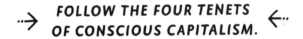

FOLLOW THE FOUR TENETS OF CONSCIOUS CAPITALISM.

They'll stead you well in investing, in business, and in life.

CHAPTER 5

5% MAX INITIAL POSITION

W HAT IS DIVERSIFICATION? Is it an outrageous motley gumbo that contains broth, lentils, jalapenos, chocolate, and bark? In order to be diversified, does one need growth, value, income, international, sector-exposure, T-bonds, ETFs, and municipals? Does such elaborate diversification stand you in good stead of being pleased by the effort?

Or, is diversification a well-concocted dish, partly due to it being kept simple and balanced along a flavor profile? Is it more like choosing your cuisine (global *or* sector-based *or* focused on market cap) and then creating a really good chicken noodle soup, or a satisfying salsa, or a perfect chocolaty treat?

If diversification means letting every instrument play at once, the conductor might feel powerful or safe, but the cacophony may not please the audience. I'll expand on this in Part III when we delve into the Six Principles of the Rule Breaker Portfolio. For now, let me rein it in and share Habit #5:

···→ **5% MAX INITIAL POSITION.** ←···

No matter how many investments you want to oversee or how many stocks your broker or ChatGPT suggests, fix on 5%. That's the maximum of your entire nest egg or portfolio to allocate to a *new* position.

My stars, if everyone had this habit, so many sorry mistakes would have been prevented, and so many more people would be reaping the rich rewards of truly investing. Instead, many newcomers hear about a stock, get excited, and put too much into it—sometimes everything. Even people with some degree of sophistication can go overboard, whether out of too much excitement or just too much focus.

When overallocated stocks drop, investors lose a lot, or all, of their investment (I've done that before), and concomitantly a lot or all of their portfolio (never done that and never will), mainly because that *was* their portfolio. When your portfolio consists of just one or a few big positions, you are asking for trouble. Even if things start well initially, an early win can be dangerous because it leads to false confidence. This false confidence can embolden you to gamble even more, loading up on a few stocks you can count on one hand. This nearly always ends badly.

But not if you habitually enter new positions with no more than $1 out of every $20 in your portfolio. Five percent. Max.

Long-time Motley Fool community member and country philosopher Tom Engle has a notable quotable that I hope you'll find instructive and hang onto. From his Kentucky abode, Tom has contributed thousands of postings to the Fool.com community forums keeping us all educated, amused, and enriched. Of making investments in riskier, enticing stocks, he has said: **"If it works, a little is all you need. And if it doesn't, a little is all you want."**

AT LEAST 20 INVESTMENTS

The numbers-inclined will already have done the math with me. If you're maximally allocating 5% of your portfolio to any single new investment, I'm implying your portfolio should contain at least 20 investments. (At least. I would probably shoot to start with 25.)

This used to be a challenging assertion. Transaction fees were high, *and* you had to buy in round lots (round numbers like 100 shares, not 102). This meant spending a lot just to open one position, let alone 20! It just wasn't feasible for those starting with a smaller amount of money.

These days, you can buy *fractional* shares (e.g., 102.3 shares), making it easier than ever to invest without paying commissions. With that in mind, you should diversify from the get-go. Habitually diversifying (Habit #5) would have greatly reduced the number of people who, over the years, have come up to me at conferences and book signings to say, "You know, I just put too much in this one or that one!"

Other than not investing at all (the #1 mistake worldwide), this one's probably mistake #2. Almost every experienced investor has a story about it. (You too?) The good news is they're talking about it, which means they've recognized it and learned a hard lesson. To avoid this common trap, don't overload on any one stock.

Twenty stocks should always be a bare minimum for a Rule Breaker portfolio. But remember Habit #1 (let your winners run!) to remind you that 5% is your maximum *initial* allocation. Not only do I want you to let your winners run, but I also have taught you Habit #2—remember?—to add up, not double down. These are important complements to Habit #5. So if one stock starts at 5% and gains value, adding to it can make it a larger position, well exceeding 5% of your portfolio.

Again, I will share more about this in Part III, but the key takeaway is that there's no single all-encompassing number for the right size of your biggest position. We all have different risk tolerances, purposes, and horizons. As a Rule Breaker, I'm more comfortable than the average person with managing an unbalanced portfolio.

I've lived long stretches of my adult life overloaded in a few stocks, but the only way that ever happened was because **they won their way to that share of my portfolio.** My greatest stocks end up being my largest holdings, having earned their allocation size through big wins. And since the winners (what do they do...?) *tend to keep on winning*, this will happen to you too. But especially if you have a diversified portfolio of multiple winners, no single stock will dominate because your big dogs will keep hitting shoulders against each other.

That's what happens in all the portfolios I've managed, whether for Motley Fool services, for my own portfolio, or for my kids. Happens every time. And it's a really great feeling: You're riding big-shouldered, for-profit public companies that do great work in this world (Habit #4) that over time will keep growing.

"STOCKS ALWAYS GO DOWN
FASTER THAN THEY GO UP..."

When we went on a rollercoaster ride in Chapter 3, it reminded me of one of my favorite lines: "Stocks always go down faster than they go up, but they always go up more than they go down." This one sentence perfectly conveys the rollercoaster analogy (I probably could have saved a few pages), and captures the wild yet ultimately oh-so-rewarding nature of Rule Breaker Investing.

It's not unusual for a Rule Breaker stock to drop 25% on a bad earnings report or forward projections. WHAM! In my investment career I have seen more one-day 25% drops than rises. Given that people fear loss three times as much as they enjoy gain, diversification and small initial allocations are crucial. You're less likely to panic out of a position when you have a bunch of others.

And you *don't* want to panic out of investing in stocks, since "they always go up more than they go down." This applies to stocks *in general*, of course. Not every stock always goes up; you will have many losers! But step back from individual stocks or sectors and look at a graph of the S&P 500. You'll see the classic movement everybody wants in their graphs—lower-left to upper-right. This trend holds true over years, across different presidencies, and even through centuries, as illustrated in Jeremy Siegel's *Stocks for the Long Run*. They always go up more than they go down.

S&P 500: 1930–2024

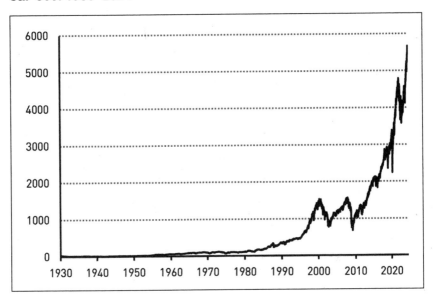

F. Scott Fitzgerald called it genius if you can keep two opposed thoughts in your head at the same time. Be a genius with me: **Stocks always go down faster than they go up, but they always go up more than they go down.** This kind of genius isn't just for showing off; it will help you maximize your returns.

By habitually starting new positions at small single-digit allocations, you do your future self a favor. That future self will surely face a day, quarter, or year when your stocks go down way faster than they were going up.

Even worse, the media will then call this a "correction…"

… that's the term! I don't know when this started, but I completely disagree that when the stock market goes down, that should be called a *correction*; invariably, they say the market is correcting only when it goes down.

Why is it correct when the stock market goes down? The idea is that the market has overshot to the upside, and so it's correct that it should return to a lower place. But by the same logic, when the market undershoots, isn't it also correcting when it *rises*?

Using "correction" only for drops contradicts the stock market's truth:

It rises two years out of every three, and over your lifetime, it will rise a great deal in value. (Rollercoaster up a mountain, anyone?) *And that's really what's correct.*

Anyway, back to our future selves, confronted by our stocks going down fast and hearing CNBC calling it a correction. These future selves sort into two types, along the classic lines of my favorite Aesop fable, "The Ant and the Grasshopper."[27]

On one side, we have the grasshoppers, living it up through the summer, thinking nothing of any such thing as... winter (?!)... as they blithely overload into hot stocks. These jumpy participants load up way more than 5% in new positions, most holding well fewer than 20 stocks. They are usually the first to panic-sell. On the other side, we have the ants, who've applied Habit #5 and put in the hard work of building diversified portfolios. Understanding the full cycle of the seasons, their prudent psychologies are much better able to accept those inevitable times when their favorite stocks go down fast.

After all, they were taught successful investing habits through all market environments by their great-grandpar-ants! They have formed the formic habit:

··⟶ 5% MAX INITIAL POSITION. ⟵··

---

27   #373 in the Perry Index, for those (is it just Perry?) keeping score at home.

CHAPTER 6

AIM FOR 60%
ACCURACY

"**W**ALL STREET SQUEAKED out a gain in 2007," the CNNMoney article started, "after what has been a particularly tough year." Despite the tough environment, that year's #1 and #2 overall performers on the Nasdaq 100 were picks I had made years earlier. Baidu, the Chinese search engine, was up 246%, and Intuitive Surgical, the leader in robot-assisted surgery, was up 239%. As 2007 ended, we proudly celebrated having held that year's gold- and silver-medal stocks from years before.

We also had 2007's #5 top stock: Amazon.com, up 139%.

And we had the #2 and #4 worst-performing Nasdaq 100 stocks, too! Starbucks was down 43% (shout-out to Lisa), and Vertex Pharmaceuticals dropped 36% in 2007.

Three big winners, two big losers... not a bad ratio. Even with just one winner—#5 Amazon, up 139%—we'd gladly accept that tasty single-stock slice sandwiched between the two losers. One big winner (+139%) mixed with two of the Nasdaq's worst (-46% and -36%) averages a 19% gain, versus overall market gains of half that.

Most people would be horrified at picking *two* of the five worst Nasdaq stocks! Most would likely invest in such a way that that could *not* happen; they'd never pick such stocks. Or if they did, they'd trade out of them to limit their downside... a classic phrase which, often, limits upside even more.

But remember, we *did* have the two top Nasdaq 100 stocks. Thus, averaging all five together, Rule Breaker Investing boasted +108% as a basket, compared to Nasdaq 100 and S&P 500 gains of 10% and 4%. I've had even better years, and many worse.

The 2007 ratio of three winners out of five picks overall perfectly reflects Habit #6:

⋯→ AIM FOR 60% ACCURACY. ←⋯

I use "accuracy" to mean whether a stock beats the market, measured by the S&P 500. If your pick *beats* the market, it's accurate. If not, it's inaccurate.

Habit #6 speaks to striving to beat the market with your portfolio. (Otherwise, why bother picking stocks? Just buy the index fund, as my brother Tom and I have said since our original bestseller *The Motley Fool Investment Guide*.) The goal is to buy great stocks and avoid enough bad ones to outperform the broad market index funds that have to buy all the stocks.

To do that, we need to find the winners and aim for accuracy.

That 60% figure is directional, not a strict target. It's more like the Pirate's Code, as Captain Jack Sparrow said: "It's really just guidelines." Habit #6 means investing with confidence that you'll get it right more often than not.

Sixty percent is comfortably aspirational, sitting between the two opposite extremes: gambling (where over time your chances of winning outright are near 0%) and the unrealistic goal of 100%.

0%, AND 100%, ACCURACY

Zero percent accuracy can be dismissed quickly. *The 0% mentality* is the penny-stock, meme stock, crypto-junk portfolio, embraced by gamblers or the uninformed. It leads to poor outcomes. Occasionally, someone might profit from sub-$1 stocks, but it's rare and unreliable. *Caveat emptor.* By now, you didn't need me to say that.

The 100% mentality, however, can entice rational people. It's supported by one of the worst lines in investing history, coming to you straight from Warren Buffett, and often cited by his fanboys and groupies:

Rule Number One: Never lose money.
Rule Number Two: Never forget Rule Number One.

Investing is not Olympic figure skating, where a single fall can cause your gold-medal hopes to come crashing down with you. Suggesting that mistakes are unthinkable, or paralyzing people from investing due to fear of mistakes, is harmful. I hope the Oracle of Omaha regrets how some have taken up these lines as their own bumper-sticker-worthy mantra, or head-nodding confirmation that Buffett has nailed it again.

You'll recall that Habit #1 from earlier starts with "Rule Number One" (go back and check... I'll be here when you return). I crafted Habit #1 this way to convey a truth distinct from the one Buffett intended. That truth:

Investing isn't Olympic figure skating; it's baseball.

BABE RUTH, TED WILLIAMS, AND YOU

In Chapter 1, I discussed home runs vs. strikeouts, concluding that the pain of loss being three times the joy of gain is untrue in investing. In fact, the joy of investment gains is infinite times the pain of loss.

I'm not the only one who can't help going back to baseball, time and again, as a metaphor. In his classic *On Becoming a Leader*, Warren Bennis strays from his topic to insert:

Babe Ruth not only set a home run record, he set a strikeout record as well. Think what a great batting average is: .400—which means a great batter fails to get a hit more than half the time. Most of the rest of us are paralyzed by our failures, large and small. We're so haunted by them, so afraid that we're going to goof again, that we become fearful of doing anything. When jockeys are thrown, they get back on the horse, because they know if they don't, their fear may immobilize them. When an F-14 pilot has to eject, he or she goes up the next day in another plane.

Expressing the same truth, after the 1986 Challenger shuttle tragedy—triggered by a cold morning launch—a TV reporter asked test pilot Chuck Yeager what NASA should do.

"I think they should wait for a warm morning," the old flying ace drawled, "and shoot off the next one." (NASA shut down the program for three years.)

Ted Williams was the last major leaguer to bat .400 for a season,[28] meaning he got a hit 40% of the time. Not 0%. Not 100%. And not 60%.[29]

Ted Williams's 1941 batting average of .406 is about .100 (100 basis points) better than today's aspirational standard of .300. Great hitters today aim for .400, which helps them exceed .300. (Few guys actually hitting .300+ today probably think, "Man, I just hope I can hit somewhere near .300!")[30]

Now back to the stock market. Just like hitters aiming for .400 hit over .300, Rule Breaker investors should aim 100 basis points higher than conventional wisdom. Conventional wisdom suggests beating the market averages would just be a coin flip, 50/50, or here: .500. Whether or not this is true,[31] aiming high is crucial. If you aim for six out of every 10 of

---

28   Possibly for all of history.

29   However, batting average is misleading, having emerged in an era of less numerical sophistication. A century ago, people seemed content mostly just to count stuff, like home runs. The cognoscenti of the time went a step further and expressed things as ratios, hence: batting average. It wasn't until the late 1970s, thanks to Bill James and others, that we broadly began to see the flaws in this measure. Batting average ignores walks, where batters obtain a free pass to first base after four bad pitches. For top hitters, this can happen a hundred times in a season. So batters in a full season would get up to bat 600 times, and walk 100 of them, and one of baseball's best known measures—batting average—would fail to account for that! This opened the door for Rule Breakers like Bill James (one of my heroes) to improve baseball.

30   Williams's achievement has arguably been overshadowed by another that caught the public's attention in the very same year: Joe DiMaggio's 56-game hitting streak. I've already asserted that getting on base (on-base percentage) is both more important *and* less recognized than getting hits (batting average), so I hasten to point out a *third* 1941 achievement far more overlooked: In this same *annus mirabilis*, Ted Williams reached base in 84 consecutive games... still to this day a record.

31   It isn't. Studies tend to show a *minority* (<50%) of stocks beat the market. But the ones that do, do it well enough, that the mean average of the market exceeds the median return of stocks.

your stock picks to beat the market, you're more likely to outperform by aiming high. Shoot for the stars, and even if you miss, you're more likely to land a moonshot.

Venture capitalists understand this well, adopting an aim-high mindset fully knowing that only a minority of their investments will win big. Chapter 1 covered the "Losing to Win" math and mentality; a Rule Breaker's "Rule Number One"—to let your winners run—is the single most important habit toward making a lot of money on the stock market. It's absolutely not about never losing, or always being right. **You have to lose to win in this world**. Aim for 60% accuracy, and let those winners do what winners do: WIN. In a world where most others won't stay around long enough to earn their 10-baggers, shoot for 100-baggers.

While we really can win without high accuracy, Rule Breaker investors nevertheless do well to favor situations where we're confident. That means habituating toward *a 60% mindset*, confident each time you swing the bat, well knowing how easily you might strike out. This 60% mindset gives you way more confidence than the 0% crowd, the crazy people rolling dice. And it will propel you ahead with way more humility than the 100% crowd—the arrogant tightrope walkers waving away their safety nets.

$\cdots\!\!\rightarrow$ **AIM FOR 60% ACCURACY.** $\leftarrow\!\!\cdots$

THE 6 HABITS OF THE RULE BREAKER INVESTOR

HABIT #1:
*RULE NUMBER ONE:
LET YOUR WINNERS RUN. HIGH.*

HABIT #2:
ADD UP, DON'T DOUBLE DOWN.

HABIT #3:
INVEST. FOR AT LEAST THREE YEARS.

HABIT #4:
*FOLLOW THE FOUR TENETS
OF CONSCIOUS CAPITALISM.*

HABIT #5:
5% MAX INITIAL POSITION.

HABIT #6:
AIM FOR 60% ACCURACY.

MAKING A LIFETIME practice of *any one* of the Six Habits of the Rule Breaker Investor will improve your investing results. (It will make the world a smarter, happier, richer place, too!)

But... *strap in*, and put all six into play? That's the dream rollercoaster ride of a lifetime (it *will* be a rollercoaster ride), leading to your own gold-medal prize of incalculable value. It's worth a lot more, by the way, than even a Wonka-tastic, hugely oversized Hershey's milk chocolate bar.

And if you're ever worried about forgetting the habits, I've laced in a mnemonic (did you notice it?), to make it easy to remember them your whole life long.

For each of the habits, the number of that habit appears somewhere in the line. Check it.

Happy memorizing.

SUMMARY OF PART I: TALE OF TWO INVESTORS

Harry's day starts with a groan, not from the sunlight peeking through the curtains, but from the overnight alerts sent from his trading app. Expected volatility at stock market open means his stop-loss orders will be triggering. On the garage elevator up to his office, he pulls out his phone to check: Yep, he just got out of his two best-performing stocks, and it looks like just in time.

Minor gains locked in. Sweet.

An advertising analyst, he spends his professional days bathed in the glow of data from the internet marketing campaigns of big-time clients. It comes in real-time, which makes Harry feel like he's on a Wall Street trading floor. His monitors sit at odd angles to each other, their juxtaposition enabling him quickly to scan the results. "Time is money" is his mantra. He's good at what he does. But he'd be even better if he wasn't more fixated on that other little screen, to his far right: his smartphone sitting in its cradle, alerting him to trades he could make.

Jake, his friend one cubicle over, knows of Harry's interest in the markets. "Patagonia's looking good today," he says.

"Patagonia's not public, fella," Harry says back, thinking Jake must have forgotten it was a private company, not one you could trade.

"I'm talking about the *client*," Jake reminds him with a smirk. Patagonia's a new account. Its "Worn Wear" campaign, promoting the longevity and re-use of quality gear—instead of always buying cheap and new—is working. "If these numbers keep rolling up," Jake goes on, "three years from now—."

"Who waits three years? I'm in and out in three minutes," Harry brags to his colleague.

Meanwhile....

Across town, Sally starts her day with a serene smile. She's just opened her brokerage statement and is scanning her retirement portfolio over coffee. Nearly two decades in, her disciplined approach shows the benefits of backing and adding to strong businesses for the long haul. Some of her initial investments have multiplied. She has a mix of funds and stocks, and while she couldn't tell you a lot about her funds, every company in her portfolio was handpicked by her with deep appreciation of their missions. It's fun to see how some positions have skyrocketed over time, especially given that Sally had never risked more than 5% on any one stock. Though she hasn't hit her aim of beating the market with 60% of them, being patient with her winners, especially her biggest holding, has greatly enriched both her portfolio and her sense of fulfillment in her choices.

At work, Sally shines as a project manager overseeing the Sunbeam Solar Array project, aiming to harness the Mojave Desert's vast solar potential to power over 300,000 homes. Unaware of the morning's market drop, her focus today is on reviewing the costs of deploying bifacial solar panels, which capture sunlight from both sides to maximize energy generation. The problem is, they're expensive. So her team is working on a public-private partnership with California, developing a comprehensive land management plan that will also serve to protect the native desert tortoise population...

... an unexpected text from Jake nudges Harry out of his trading trance. "Charity event for green initiatives tonight. Free food, and who knows, maybe Patagonia's ethos will rub off on you," Jake teases. Reluctantly, Harry agrees, more enticed by the promise of gourmet canapés than any change of heart.

At the fundraiser, sponsored by the Sunbeam Solar Array project, Harry finds himself out of his element. His market banter falls flat amidst discussions on sustainability and solar panels. It's here, by the silent auction table, that he bumps into Sally—literally, as he backpedals from a conversation about desert tortoises into her. She'd been about to make a bid.

Sally looks up: There's something about this stranger—maybe the sharp suit in a crowd of eco-conscious attire, or the genuine embarrassment in his eyes. "Well, hello to you too," she says, smiling. "Is that your way of making a bid?"

Harry, caught off guard by her gaze, manages a sheepish grin. "It's a silent auction. I was... trying to see your number. *Silently.* I'm all about numbers."

"Hi, All About Numbers. I'm Sally," she extends her hand, then points to her nametag. "I work on the Sunbeam project. It's a big part of why I'm here tonight. We're hoping to raise awareness and support for our sustainable energy initiatives."

She pauses, studying him for a moment, then says: **"What's the most meaningful thing you've ever invested in?"**

Huh. Good question. Idle happy-hour banter, probably. Unless you really started to think about it....

PART

THE 6 TRAITS OF THE RULE BREAKER STOCK

BACK IN 1999 I shared the Six Traits I look for in stocks. *Rule Breakers, Rule Makers* was a hit, a bestseller.

But publishing your ideas as a young enthusiast lacks one thing: Results. Investing is measured in years, in decades. All we can do initially is say what we're planning to do, go out there on the field, and do it. Do it, and wait: Days. Months. Years.

It's now over 25 years later. Decades have happened. The market, a "voting machine" in the short term, has performed its long-term function as a "weighing machine."[32] Those Six Traits making up my game plan since the late 1990s have enabled me to find many of the great stocks of the past 25 years—find them early, and often.

Peter Lynch made a career identifying 10-baggers, stocks rising ten times or more in value during his 13 years of managing Fidelity Magellan. I aimed for that, too. Over 20 years, picking three stocks a month, I've scored 64 10+-baggers.

Seeing 64 stock picks rise tenfold or more, knowing they've found their way into the portfolios of those who followed my recommendations, has given me incalculable joy. Full stop.

But what excites me even more is the 100-baggers. Seven of them, so far.

They possess the traits. It's Part II of *Rule Breaker Investing*.

Let's look at what keeps working, year after year, in the best stocks.

---

32 While this classic metaphor doesn't seem to appear *verbatim* in Benjamin Graham's writings, Warren Buffett attributes it to him, saying he often used it in his classes and lectures.

CHAPTER 7

TOP DOG AND FIRST-MOVER

"If you want to succeed you should strike out on new paths, rather than travel the worn paths of accepted success."

—JOHN D. ROCKEFELLER

J ERRY GARCIA ISN'T found in many investing books, but the co-founder of The Grateful Dead is here in mine for delivering one of the great visionary investing and business lines of all time:

We were never trying to be the best at what we do. We were trying to be the only ones doing what we were doing.[33]

As we begin Part II's first and most important chapter, let's savor the greatness of his Gratefulness. And recognize at the same time how well Garcia's line dovetails with this chapter's epigraph from John D. Rockefeller, the wealthiest and most influential man of his generation. The two never met (Rockefeller died in 1937; Garcia was born in 1942) and had obvious differences. But in this way of thinking, they are united.

---

33 The line may actually have come from Grateful Dead promoter Bill Graham, not Jerry. As I can't even name any of the band's songs, I'll let others debate the provenance.

Because this is how Rule Breakers think. This is what a Rule Breaker does. It disrupts. It creates industries. It shocks the world. It is the:

...→ **TOP DOG AND FIRST-MOVER IN AN IMPORTANT, EMERGING INDUSTRY.** ←..

Trait #1 of Rule Breaker stocks is number one for a reason. This trait is a powerful filter and time-saver. If you take nothing else from Part II, remember this lesson: Most great stocks of every era are top dogs and first-movers in important, emerging industries. By focusing your research on these, you're fishing in a stocked pond (pun intended). In this little pond, ignored by many, swim the great stocks of the next generation.

For companies in emergent industries to attain Rule Breaker positioning is incredibly impressive. It's no small feat to transform a garage idea into a public company leading the way with the next great solution that will disrupt the powers that be!

It's not just impressive; that pole positioning itself becomes a competitive advantage, like in an auto race. Bloomberg, CNBC, and the financial press all want to talk about you, boosting your brand recognition. Top talent wants to work for you, and the best venture capitalists want to fund you. These factors, along with technology advantage, speed of execution, and visionary leadership, don't just help a company become the top dog and first-mover; they *sustain* it. That's how Amazon becomes Amazon, Tesla Tesla. Top dogs and first-movers like Facebook, Nvidia, and Netflix can become self-fulfilling prophecies.

To scan for this trait, break it into two parts: the company itself (**top dog and first-mover**), and the industry it creates or operates in (**important and emerging**). Let's take them in reverse order, industries first.

Look at lists of the great stocks over a 30-year period, and you'll see many credited with starting their own industries. They were doing something important, and emerging. Check the table on the next page for the 30 years from January 1995 to December 2024, focusing especially on companies with asterisks next to their names—the ones that went public (IPO'd) during this period.

Best performing stocks in the S&P 500 (January 1995–December 2024)

Company	IPO date	30-year total return	Annualized return
Nvidia*	1/22/1999	369,804%	37.2%
Amazon.com*	5/15/1997	292,422%	33.5%
Monster Beverage*	8/18/1995	268,294%	30.8%
NVR	6/17/1986	148,608%	27.6%
Texas Pacific Land	5/29/1975	125,866%	26.9%
Axon Enterprise*	6/7/2021	111,196%	34.6%
Apple	12/12/1980	86,134%	25.3%
Netflix*	5/23/2002	82,703%	34.6%
Jabil*	5/5/1998	73,864%	28.1%
Ross Stores	8/8/1985	56,547%	23.5%
Pool*	10/13/1995	51,689%	23.8%
Biogen	9/17/1991	46,798%	22.8%
Altria Group	7/2/1985	46,505%	22.7%
Gilead Sciences	1/22/1992	43,449%	22.5%
O'Reilly Automotive	4/22/1993	38,225%	21.9%
ResMed*	6/2/1995	36,276%	22.0%
TJX Companies	11/17/1965	35,438%	21.6%
Cognizant Technology Solutions*	6/19/1998	33,851%	24.5%
Copart	3/17/1994	31,154%	21.1%
Deckers Outdoor	10/21/1993	29,145%	20.8%
Johnson Controls International	10/11/1965	26,722%	20.5%
Old Dominion Freight Line	10/24/1991	25,418%	20.3%
Fair Isaac	7/31/1987	25,401%	20.3%
Tesla*	6/29/2010	25,320%	46.4%
Intuitive Surgical*	6/13/2000	24,788%	25.2%
Tractor Supply	2/17/1994	24,188%	20.1%
Regeneron Pharmaceuticals	4/2/1991	23,644%	20.0%
Amphenol	11/08/1991	21,109%	19.6%
Costo Wholesale	11/27/1985	21,089%	19.5%
Microsoft	3/13/1986	17,788%	18.9%

Source: YCharts and Charlie Bilello.

In Chapter 4 I introduced the Snap Test: "If I snapped my fingers and the company disappeared, would anyone notice? Would anyone care?" This is a great way to evaluate the importance of what a company does. An innovator operating in an important, emerging industry will easily pass the Snap Test. (If not, it might still be worth researching, but it's not a Rule Breaker.)

Important and emerging industries aren't always well known to consumers. Copart, an online auction company for salvaged and used vehicles, and ResMed, a pioneer in CPAP (continuous positive airway pressure) machines for sleep apnea, are prime examples. Most people wouldn't recognize these corporate names, yet they operate in significant, under-addressed markets. These Rule Breakers, driven by technology, may not have the consumer appeal of Netflix or Apple, but they are integral to important and emerging industries—just as Netflix and Apple were once, before them.

New technology is being developed and deployed faster than ever. The internet was adopted faster than the telephone, and artificial intelligence is being adopted faster than the internet. More Rule Breakers are headed your way, likely more than ever before. That's why it's so rewarding to watch for new technologies that solve old problems or create new possibilities.

In the 1967 film *The Graduate*, a family friend buttonholes young Benjamin Braddock (played by Dustin Hoffman) to convey to him the future in a single word: "Plastics." At the time, the plastics industry represented the cutting edge of technological advancement and economic opportunity. Humor and social commentary aside, a family friend these days might just as urgently pull you aside with:

"AI."

"Genomics."

"Sustainability."

"Quantum."

"Blockchain."

"Space."

"Robots."

The future stretches before us, a boundless horizon of endless possibilities and uncharted territories. Rule Breaker investors do well to keep our eyes focused right there on the edges.

But the Snap Test reminds us not to be too edgy. As a younger man, I was excited about nanotechnology and looked for Rule Breakers that might be *overnight* successes in the early 2000s. Twenty years later, I'm still waiting for morning to break. (Cold fusion, anyone?) Fortunately, I didn't waste too much time or capital on these pursuits because no nanotech company would clearly be missed if you snapped your fingers and it disappeared.[34] **The Snap Test is a great guide for important and emerging.**

Before we move on to "top dog and first-mover," I want to address the inevitable exceptions that arise when one creates lists of Habits, Traits, and Principles ("Rules" we might call them... ironically, from a Rule Breaker).

Look again at those top 30-year stocks. The number three performer is Monster Beverage Corporation. Many might not see energy drinks as the next big thing. The debut of Red Bull in Austria on April 1, 1987 was not necessarily a Glendowerian moment ("I say the earth did shake when I was born").[35] It wasn't technology-driven, on a par with the graphic processing units of Nvidia. But Rule Breakers aren't always about technology. Even "important" can mean different things. (Did you see Costco on that list?)

The rise of energy drinks may not rival the internet or electric self-driving cars in importance, but it reflects a shift toward increased productivity and an always-on lifestyle. Red Bull (still a private company to this day) and its American public company competitor—Monster Beverage Corp.—transformed beverage consumption and influenced cultural norms around work and performance, symbolizing a broader cultural trend toward optimization and efficiency in daily life.

Or if you disagree, no need to have bought the stock!

---

34   Or shrunk to nano-size. I figured there was a joke in here somewhere but couldn't find it well enough so I asked ChatGPT, and it came back with: "Why is the nanotech industry considered so small? Because its market size is literally of nano proportions! Investors need a microscope just to see their returns!"

35   Though as a Fool I'd like to point out that Red Bull debuted on April Fool's Day!

I sure am glad we did, though, in January 2009.[36] (Still holding!) I may not drink energy drinks, nor is Monster Beverage Corp. the most obvious example of Trait #1. But Trait #1 isn't the only Rule Breaker trait. And Monster Beverage, even though we didn't get it from its earliest days, has been a wonderful 15+-year holding for Rule Breakers everywhere.

Important and emerging industries with their bright and beautiful colors are the dominant species swimming around so alluringly in that pond stocked with each era's next great stocks. The Snap Test helps you choose the right bait and tackle to reel in the stocks that anchor a trophy-winning portfolio.

All this talk of ponds and energy drinks is making me thirsty. Speaking of drinks....

THE COLA TEST

Having now considered important, emerging industries, I want to focus again on the first half of Trait #1: top dog and first-mover. This is easier to identify once you've observed important, emerging industries. You're now simply asking which is the company leading this race. There's your top dog.

Sticking with canines, an old saying goes: "If you're not the lead husky, the view never changes." Lead-husky companies are driven by dreamers and visionaries. When investors let these lead huskies guide our sleds, they take us to places no one had gone before, to pots of gold behind trees no one else knew about.

Think again of Rockefeller's worn paths. The founding teams behind every generation's Rule Breakers unchain their dog teams and sleds, setting off—it seems crazy!—into the hinterlands, striking out, forging genius new paths. I'm using "genius" intentionally here, alluding to another favorite line always to be kept in mind, this from the 19th-century philosopher Arthur Schopenhauer:

---

36 Motley Fool Rule Breakers pick, January 21, 2009—though technically I recommended Hansen Natural (HNSN). It had been the previous decade's top stock (speaking to Trait #3). It decided to rename itself Monster Beverage Corporation in 2012 (speaking to Trait #4—we'll get there).

Talent hits a target no one else can hit.
Genius hits a target no one else can see.

So top dogs aren't hard to spot, once you focus on real innovators driving societal change. But there's more to be said about first-movers, specifically *how* they move.

Most top dogs, as Rule Breakers disrupting Goliaths in established industries, are first-movers. I'm not insisting that you always follow the first-mover. MySpace preceded Facebook; I'm aware of the old cliché that dismisses pioneers, rather than champions them, because they are the ones on the front lines "with arrows in their backs" that others step over. But often, top dogs like Spotify (on-demand music streaming) and Square (small-business payment platform) were the first-movers *at scale* in the industries they helped create.

But *how* a company moves is more important than *that* it moves. Knee-jerk reactions are great when helping to snag a valuable domain name, but not so great when they lead to hastily recalling a product, sparking a PR disaster. How a dancer dances matters more than just dancing. Similarly, *how* a first-mover moves is critical, and can be assessed by an additional test.

Enter The Cola Test.

For me to like a stock, it doesn't have to pass this test. But for me to love a stock, it does. The greatest Rule Breakers of every era pass both the Snap Test and the Cola Test.

Back to the Jerry Garcia line that opened this chapter, about being the only ones doing what you're doing. *When I spot a promising company and can't find a Pepsi playing rival to its Coke, that's when I get really excited.* So here it is:

The Cola Test

Is the company you're evaluating *the only one doing what it's doing*?
Can you find no Pepsi to its Coke?

For instance, Amazon.com. There has never been a company that serves as a clear analog to Amazon. From its earliest days selling books online[37] to adding Amazon Web Services in 2006 and competing with Netflix in streaming video, Amazon has always stood alone. If Amazon were Coke, who's the Pepsi? It's one thing to grasp the future of e-commerce and move first, but it's much stronger when you are the lead husky, with others only staring at your flanks. Rule Breaker companies that ace the Cola Test keep exploring and moving into positions where there's no competition. Our stocked ponds look like wide-open blue oceans!

Blue-ocean opportunities for Amazon and its ilk succeed because as talented as many competitors may be, they can't see the genius's vision. Founder Jeff Bezos wasn't trying to be the best; he was trying to be the only one.

There are three i's in every cycle, Warren Buffett once wrote. "First come the innovators, who see opportunities that others don't. Then come the imitators, who copy what the innovators have done. And then come the idiots, whose avarice undoes the very innovations they are trying to use to get rich." Ignore the imitators and the idiots and stay focused on the innovators, *who see opportunities that others don't.*

That's how Apple became Apple, and Shopify Shopify.

SNAP COLA

Rule Breaker Trait #1 combines the Snap Test and the Cola Test. As a mnemonic, I offer you the catchy phrase Snap Cola—a brand that doesn't exist to my knowledge, but might be a pretty great entrant in the energy drink industry. Amazon.com, top dog and first-mover in the important, emerging industry of *e-commerce* (and later, others), is a prime example of Snap Cola.

Snap Cola companies possess a devastating 1–2 punch:

(1) Snap: They have early on achieved huge importance and relevance.

---

37 I still mouse over my vintage "Earth's Biggest Bookseller" Amazon.com mousepad.

(2) Cola: They are the only ones doing what they're doing.

Snap Cola companies are the bedrocks of any great investment portfolio. A few of these over a lifetime can provide all the wealth we need. Snap Cola companies provide the Monster Energy that powers our Rule Breaker portfolios.[38]

Quick practice for you: Let's go back to Apple, always an accessible example. Does it pass *the Cola Test* for you? Did it always?

I'd say through most of its first 20 years, Apple largely played Pepsi to Microsoft's Coke, coming to a head with the iconic Mac vs. PC showdown ads of the mid 2000s. However, the launch of the iPod and later the iPhone in 2007 significantly differentiated Apple's product set. Apple's culture, design philosophy, and brand had always been unique, but now it had a product suite positioning it finally as *the only one doing what it was doing*. (Today, Samsung is Apple's Pepsi.) Apple passing the Cola Test was what I needed to see and so in 2008, I finally picked it.[39] Snap Cola City!

Another example is Alphabet. In the early 2000s, Google's search engine began to overtake Yahoo!, becoming so easy-to-use and dominant that you were hard-put to find any Pepsi resembling its Coke. Ask Jeeves? Bing? My longtime Motley Fool sidekick Tim Beyers has a great eye for Rule Breakers, and suggested we pick it, which we did in May 2008. That was still two years before the company would launch Google X (its incubator aiming at moonshots). Today, Alphabet spans widely varying industries—from autonomous driving (Waymo) and the biology of aging (Calico), to high-altitude balloon internet (formerly Project Loon) and AI breakthroughs like DeepMind's AlphaGo, which in 2016 ousted the world's greatest champion at humanity's oldest board game. Snap Cola.

Tesla. Facebook. Intuitive Surgical. Adobe. Netflix. Axon Enterprise. Salesforce. All are top dogs and first-movers in important, emerging industries. These Snap Cola examples are not just correct answers on a *Rule Breaker Investing* Chapter 7 pop quiz. These Rule Breakers have offered the best investment returns of this generation, and all seven are

---

38   Any puns in this sentence, as well as the entire book, are free of charge.

39   $4.88 on 1/18/2008, for Motley Fool Stock Advisor. (Still holding!) Note this was years and years after Apple started. I know many with a much earlier cost basis; I hope they're still holding too.

stocks I picked early and continue to hold years later. They help power market-beating results that some academic observers will dismiss as luck.

If "Snap Cola" is too silly for you, here's another way I've expressed Trait #1:

I try to find excellence, buy excellence, and add to excellence over time. I sell mediocrity. That's how I invest.

You can too. Especially now that you know Trait #1, the first and most important sign of a Rule Breaker stock:

$\dashrightarrow$ **TOP DOG AND FIRST-MOVER IN AN IMPORTANT, EMERGING INDUSTRY.** $\dashleftarrow$

CHAPTER 8

SUSTAINABLE COMPETITIVE ADVANTAGE

I F YOU'RE GOING to buy a stock to hold for *at least* three years, if not three decades, then you'd better be buying into:

···→ *SUSTAINABLE COMPETITIVE ADVANTAGE.* ←···

Rule Breaker Trait #2 helps you look beyond the next quarter's earnings and even the next year's results. Focus on the company itself, not just its stock or valuation.

While many, especially professionals, fixate on stock tickers and price charts, your goal should be to understand a company's competitive advantages. This approach emphasizes *business*-focused investing. Like a venture capitalist, spend your time thinking through how this company wins, beats its competition, wins for customers, wins for investors.

Trait #2 makes you a student of the most important game in investing: determining who will win *sustainably*. Not next week's ballgame, or even this whole season, but who will rack up the most Ws over the next ten years.

Seems challenging, no? Most of us, myself included, do not have MBA degrees. We didn't spend a lot of time in college—this was not covered in my literature classes—asking, "Who wins in business over the long haul?" But we are all consumers! You don't need academic expertise to notice that Chick-fil-A, Walt Disney, Apple, and that multi-generational corner store or family-owned brewery in your hometown have all been around for a long time, competing successfully against other wannabes.

The key to examining competitive advantage lies in thinking through why this is. And the benefits of finding competitive advantage lead to what Einstein supposedly called the eighth wonder of the world, compounding returns/interest/benefits, what have you.[40]

Much has been made of the power of compounding *outside* of investing. James Clear in *Atomic Habits* talks about tiny changes, remarkable results. Tiago Forte's *Building a Second Brain* discusses organizing your digital life to generate compounding interest from your thoughts. Compounding occurs in many areas besides money, like trust and relationships. A rich marriage, a gift to all those who surround it, is a beautiful example of compounding effects over time.

That said, this book *is* actually focused on the very real benefits of compounding financial returns over time—specifically not interrupting or throwing away those benefits. Thus, you should highly prize and seek out sustainable competitive advantage.

CHEATING

I wrote above that you don't need academic expertise to become aware of and interested in sustainable competitive advantage. But you can delve much deeper on this topic than I will here. Michael Porter's classic *Competitive Advantage* is just one of many books he's written on the subject. Clayton Christensen, one of my academic heroes, formed his theories about disruptive innovation largely by examining competitive advantage. He noticed the irony that the larger companies get, the *more vulnerable* they become, as they focus on sustaining their advantages while upstarts (I call them Rule Breakers) quietly revolutionize their industry from the ground up. This is a much deeper topic than I will cover here.

But I also don't believe you need to overthink this. My Six Traits are

---

40 Einstein never actually said this.

not individual litmus tests each requiring a chemistry lab to produce; they are a framework. They work in concert together. Like a concert, you can hear it, see it, come to love and know it, without needing to read the sheet music.

In fact, my favorite short treatment of sustainable competitive advantage comes from a classic Seth Godin piece called "Cheating." An expert marketer and iconoclastic thinker, Seth is also a creative and humorous writer. His 2002 book *Purple Cow* posits that to stand out in a crowded market, businesses must be remarkable, like a hypothetical purple cow among a field of ordinary ones, emphasizing that uniqueness and innovation are key to attracting attention and achieving success. In a one-page chapter called "Cheating," Seth writes:

> Starbucks is cheating. The coffee bar phenomenon was invented by them, and now whenever we think coffee, we think Starbucks. Vanguard is cheating. Their low-cost index funds make it impossible for a full-service broker to compete. Amazon.com is cheating. Their free shipping and huge selection give them an unfair advantage over the neighborhood store. Google is cheating. They learned from the mistakes of the first-generation portals and they don't carry the baggage of their peers.... To their entrenched (but nervous) competitors, these companies appear to be cheating because they're not playing by the rules.[41]

He closes by asking his business readers: "Why aren't you cheating?"[42]

Many of my favorite companies and stock picks are cheating. To be clear, this is a playful term of endearment, not actual (immoral) cheating.[43] "Cheating" is enjoying and exploiting your natural competitive advantages,

---

41 *Hmmmmmm...* sound familiar?

42 It's worth noting that Seth wrote this in 2002. If you had bought these stocks back then, you'd be extremely happy 20+ years later. To my point about the value of sustainable competitive advantage, *quod erat demonstrandum.*

43 And to make it even clearer, Seth followed up fully against the *real* cheating with a wonderful blog entitled "Cheating" (August 18, 2020): seths.blog/2020/08/cheating

"unfair" in that only you possess them. It's what great athletes do to their peers.

In business, Netflix cheated Blockbuster Video out of existence, taking a better business model (digital vs. bricks-and-mortar) and converting Blockbuster's unhappy renters, used to paying late fees, into happy *subscribers*. Subscription itself was an internet business model that Blockbuster couldn't employ. Completely unfair and cheating of Reed Hastings to do that!

Marvel has been cheating. Starting in earnest in the 1990s, its decades-old treasure trove of proprietary comic-book characters marched out of their yellowing pages and onto the Hollywood silver screen. Even secondary characters most people had never heard of, like Guardians of the Galaxy, became billion-dollar properties. Totally underhanded!

And Tesla is another cheater, leveraging its visionary head start in battery technology and software integration to start an electric-vehicle revolution. Elon Musk was already supporting his fleet with a nationwide network of superchargers before most other automakers had announced their first electric models. Scalawag!

Competitive advantage springs from others of our Six Traits. Trait #5 (strong consumer appeal) conveys the benefits of greatly pleasing customers (which greatly displeases competitors). Trait #4 speaks to having visionary leadership: "We have Jeff Bezos (or Michael Jordan). You don't. We win." And Trait #1's advocacy for top dogs and first-movers is foundational in a world where new technology waves surge and create their own momentum—yet another contributor to competitive advantage. "Once a new technology rolls over you, if you're not part of the steamroller, you're part of the road," Silicon Valley visionary Stewart Brand once wrote.

If you want to win, invent the game, and make all your competitors play it. Cheating!

MORE SUSTAINABLE COMPETITIVE ADVANTAGES

When I first set down my traits in our 1999 book *Rule Breakers, Rule Makers*, I focused on four types of sustainable competitive advantage, and I still agree with them all. I highlighted:

1. **Business momentum**: Dynamics like network effects take hold. From the start, eBay got big fast because every seller attracted more buyers, and every buyer attracted more sellers. It was playing its own game, and now, 30 years later, the only clear Pepsi to eBay's Coke would be Amazon Marketplace, which later tried to replicate what Pierre Omidyar started. Similarly, Facebook grew so rapidly it became immediately famous and global.

2. **Patent protection**: Especially critical for industries like pharmaceuticals, where an approved drug gets 20 years of legal protection against copycats. But it's not just FDA approval. Hardware makers like Apple and Samsung, and software giants like Microsoft and Oracle (and Apple), own extensive patent portfolios that protect their R&D investments.

3. **Visionary leadership**: Already mentioned, and I'll discuss more in Chapter 10.

4. **Inept competition**: Companies thrive not just due to their own strengths, but also because of their rivals' failures to innovate or adapt. Examples since I wrote that chapter in 1999 are legion— Apple had Nokia, Google had Yahoo, Facebook had MySpace, Uber had taxis. The familiarity of these stories today underscores why this fourth type of advantage remains worth highlighting.

I've since come across many other forms of sustainable competitive advantage. I didn't know what conscious capitalism was in 1999; now, I believe that companies practicing conscious capitalism will win most of the profit share in most industries over the next 25 years. I hope Chapter 4 helped you see why. Purpose-powered companies regularly outperform their aimless competitors. Conscious culture, another of the four tenets, is where innovation will live and breathe... or, lacking it, suffocate and wither away. As an amateur cultural anthropologist myself, who contributed to making The Motley Fool a winning workplace culture in its time, I recognize the rich soil that corporate culture can be, and I actively seek it in the companies whose stocks I purchase.

Did I miss something in these lists? I bet I did; if you're already pointing out one I'm missing, my work is done here. The key is to care and pay attention.

Sustainable competitive advantages are powerful and undergird our greatest investments. They can be subtle or seemingly small! Take having employees who smile (when the competition doesn't). Tony Hsieh turned his shoe company, Zappos, into a billion-dollar enterprise bought by Amazon. His understanding of the power of happy employees made Zappos the envy of its industry, and for a time you could even sign up just to take tours of its offices. (I once did a tour of the Ben & Jerry's headquarters in Vermont, but mainly for the ice cream.)

Tony was asked once, "How do you get all your employees to smile?"

He dead-panned, "Easy. We just hire the applicants who smile!" Beyond being a funny punchline, this was authentic. I see this kind of *esprit de corps* enlivening the fast-moving drive-thru lines across America's Chick-fil-As. The fast-food business is not one with traditionally high standards for hospitality and deportment. That's part of the reason I think Chick-fil-A is so dominant. The former chief marketing officer of the company once said, "When I ask Chick-fil-A restaurant operators what business they are in, none ever say 'fast food restaurant.' Instead, I hear responses like, 'We are a leadership academy masquerading as a fast food restaurant.'" And even if that's a bit fluffy or not fully realized, *that* it might even be partially true, or be something people say, is, ipso facto, the point.

DARK CLOUDS I CAN SEE THROUGH

Detecting competitive advantage where others see vulnerability or weakness sets up the most lucrative investing opportunities. I call these situations "dark clouds I can see through."

Dark clouds symbolize a strongly negative prevailing view of a stock—big, dark, and evident to everyone. Picture a storm cloud bursting with lightning and rain directly over Charlie Brown's head. This represents broadly pessimistic sentiment: Investing in this company is not going to work out, and everyone can see it.

Seeing through these clouds means having unique insight. Based on your research and experience, you believe people are missing something.

You don't think those clouds are so dark, and you can see through them more clearly than the next fool (small "f").

The key is, you're in the minority. You have to show humility in the face of so much confidence on the other side. You may very well be wrong. But you maintain your hunch that the outcome will be better, even wildly so, than the bad tidings issuing from the doom-and-gloom crowd.

If you're right when the world bets against you, these are the situations that make Rule Breaker investors the most money. As you keep holding that investment, the world will slowly realize it was wrong, and you were right. Some early skeptics become converts and begin to buy the stock. As more buyers come flooding in over the months and years, that stock climbs the proverbial wall of worry (a phrase used to visualize a generationally great stock's rise from lower-left to upper-right). From the outset, there was a huge, prevailing negative perception—a big, dark cloud—so there are a lot of converts and dollars to be made over the years.

A few examples:

(1) E-commerce in the 90s

Let me re-reference a quick story included in "Your Parents Were Wrong" from Chapter O: Rewind to 1996 or 1997. I was on CNN Headline News. They introduced me, saying, "Coming back, we'll have David Gardner from something called The Motley Fool. *He thinks you* will *give your credit cards over the internet.* Back after this." That was the dark cloud at the time. The mainstream media doubted that consumers would feel safe giving out their credit cards to buy things online. I was invited on to be the Fool who believed people *would* (which did sound scary to some).

We'd started our site on AOL (often dismissed as "chat rooms") and invested early in companies like Amazon, eBay, and AOL. We were internet adoption mega-bulls! The value of being on that side of the trade (for decades) has been immense, even despite the dot-com bust in 2001, which temporarily crushed these investments. Amazon, which I still hold, exemplifies this. E-commerce and the internet's broad power and potential, taken for granted today, formed a massive dark cloud I could see through. The competitive advantage for firms built on the internet has been enduringly sustainable.

(2) "Walmart will crush _____"

As Rule Breakers emerge and attract attention, the common view is that the Rule Maker in their industry will crush them. It happens: Promising upstarts have been trampled. (Napster, anyone? MySpace?) But neither Napster nor MySpace truly exemplified our six Rule Breaker traits.[44] True-blue Rule Breakers, though they seem nutty, are tougher than most people think, and some become nuts impossible to crack.

I saw this happen twice with Walmart. Due to its size and power, Walmart was regularly seen by the media, analysts, and short sellers as capable of crushing any competitor. From 1999–2005, this was a prevalent belief concerning Amazon. Amazon was always said not to be making money, and once Walmart fully embraced e-commerce, Amazon would be doomed. (Nope.)

Then, it was Netflix facing the same dire prediction back in the DVD rental era. Walmart began offering video rentals in its megastores; customers could pick up and drop off DVDs while shopping. The idea was that with Walmart competing head-to-head, Netflix's red-envelopes-through-the-mail model was doomed.

The dark clouds I could see through here were twofold, a beautiful double-whammy. First, despite their size, large companies like Walmart struggle to compete in niches against focused, internet-savvy competitors. Second, the value of visionary "smartest guys in the room" founders like Jeff Bezos and Reed Hastings is incalculable (cf. Chapter 10); Walmart, once a Rule Breaker itself under Sam Walton, had no comparable leadership. Note that Walmart has done just fine since the mid-2000s; the business has grown and its stock too (up five times in value—in line with market averages)...

---

44   I call them Faker Breakers.

... but, over the past 20 years, Amazon (+10,000%) and Netflix (+52,000%) have spectacularly scored the dazzling gains available to investors who can see through dark clouds.

(3) Fads, like Starbucks or superhero movies

Writing off something as a fad creates many dark clouds. When Starbucks went public in 1992, many dismissed coffeehouses as a passing trend. American history lacked any precedent for a coffeehouse revolution, so Starbucks was routinely written off... years before Ling's Money Thing was a thing!

A similar misperception surrounded superhero movies. After Sony's first smash hit *Spider-Man* movie in 2002, market critics argued that the superhero craze would be fleeting, once again. Doubters pointed back to the 1980s Batman and Superman franchises petering out. A dark cloud hung over Marvel stock as it dropped in the summer of 2002, forecasting that Tobey Maguire might not be spinning too many more webs around Manhattan. Helping me see through this dark cloud was Marvel's immense potential to free its characters from the old unprofitable medium where they'd been imprisoned (comic books) to the lucrative silver screen. I picked the stock in June 2002, and remember following Marvel characters' ongoing box-office receipts (from Spider-Man to Hulk to later Iron Man) with an avidity I have rarely given any investments. As I said earlier, Marvel was "cheating." Not long after, Disney recognized the potential and bought us out of our Marvel shares, which we exchanged for Disney stock. Even with the mighty Mouse faltering badly in recent years, that initial investment in Marvel, through Disney, has risen 62 times in value.

Additional examples abound, whether we're talking about Pokemon or Crocs. These products and the firms behind them are easily written off as fads, yet their brands and fan bases run much deeper, creating remarkably sustainable competitive advantages.

If this is starting to sound like me bragging about some of my best stock picks, that's kind of my point: **When you find a dark cloud you can see through, and you're right, and you hold, these are the investments**

that lead to early retirement and multi-generational wealth. As I mentioned earlier, for the biggest Rule Breakers, you really do want skeptics *in droves*, who will eventually become converts, which is what powers your gains.

So, yeah: People did give their credit cards over the internet.

From cheating to dark clouds, much of the analysis of competitive advantage draws on the right side of the brain,[45] is inherently subjective, and *can change over time.* There is no definitive way to *check this box* and be certain it exists for the company you're considering.

As the cliché goes, "It's about the journey, not the destination." Your focus on Trait #2 should be inquisitive, attentive, and where appropriate, confirming or denying. And when you think you've found a dark cloud you can see through, grin, saddle up, and prepare for what may be a long, wild ride.

Remember, as you ask such questions and noodle on their answers, you are one of a tiny minority of market participants that day who actually cares about:

···> SUSTAINABLE COMPETITIVE ADVANTAGE. <···

---

45   Great book! Thank you, Betty Edwards.

CHAPTER 9

STELLAR PAST PRICE APPRECIATION

WILLIAM O'NEIL WROTE one of the poorer books in investing history. In *How To Make Money in Stocks*, the founder of *Investor's Business Daily* advocated selling any stock that drops 7% or more in value. Investors need to minimize losses, he counseled his trading clientele; when any position goes against you to the tune of -7% or more, sell now, ask questions later. This was his "sell discipline" (cf. Chapter 2). Having graduated Part I, you can probably guess what I think of that advice.[46]

William O'Neil also wrote one of the better books in investing history. It's the same book! My investing life has been immeasurably enriched by O'Neil's work, and I credit him for Trait #3, which I have used to great effect for decades. It's one of the two Rule Breaker Traits based not on the company, but the stock. And it works so well because—you guessed it—it Foolishly runs opposite to our instincts. *Before* we buy a stock, we want to see:

··→ STELLAR PAST PRICE APPRECIATION. ←··

---

46 We had the pleasure of meeting him in person (*Investor's Business Daily* and The Motley Fool have been business partners) and found him to be a gentleman. He did reiterate all of his same points about selling and felt that we at the Fool didn't have discipline.

Of course, we even more want to see that *after* we buy a stock! But with Rule Breakers, you're more likely to experience stellar price appreciation *if you've already seen it beforehand.*

O'Neil's research into the greatest winners of past decades revealed that the best stocks tend to rise and then rise again. Looked at one way, the insight is blindingly obvious. But given the conventional wisdom to "buy low" on "dips" and avoid yesterday's hot stock, William O'Neil unearthed one of the investing world's great discoveries.

In a world where most investors build their watchlist from stocks making 52-week lows, O'Neil's great discovery was to favor those hitting 52-week *highs.*

Let's dig in.

THE ONES THAT GOT AWAY...?

Take a look at these seven stock graphs (alphabetical by company name):

Amazon.com (AMZN): Three months (June 9, 1997–September 9, 1997)

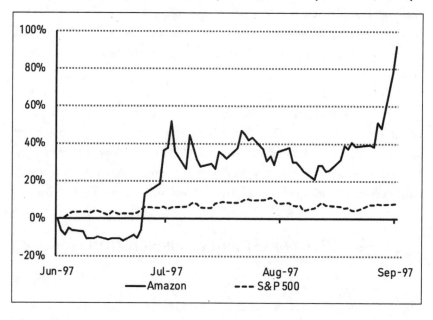

Apple (AAPL): Nine months (April 18, 2007–January 18, 2008)

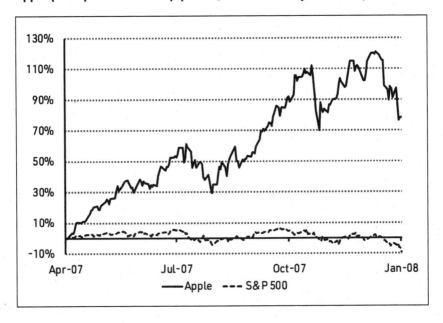

Booking Holdings (BKNG): Four months (January 1, 2004–May 1, 2004)

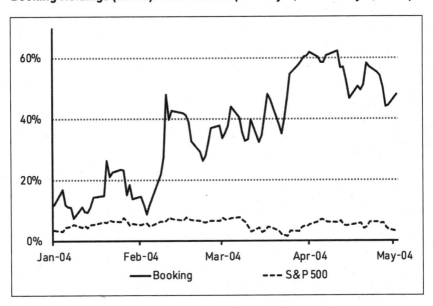

Intuitive Surgical (ISRG): Five months (October 16, 2004–March 16, 2005)

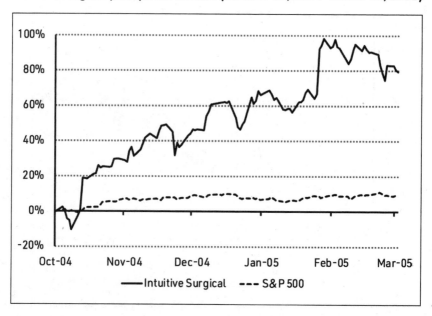

MercadoLibre(MELI):Threemonths(November18,2008–February18,2009)

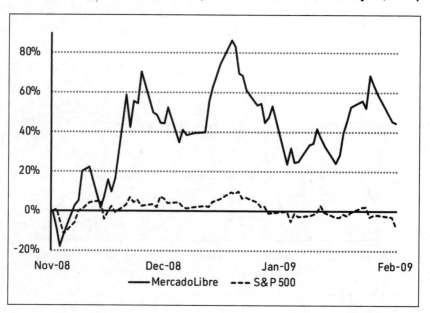

Nvidia (NVDA): Seven months (September 15, 2004–April 15, 2005)

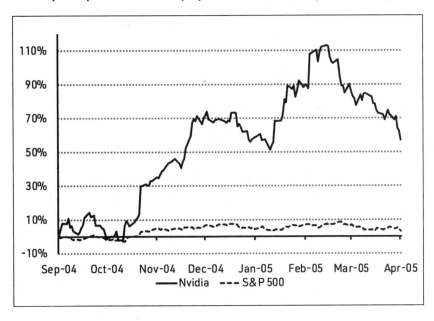

Tesla (TSLA): Three months (August 23, 2011–November 23, 2011)

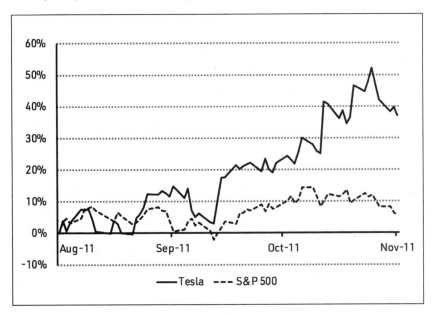

Looking at these graphs, you see stocks gaining 30–90% over three to nine months.[47] Other books might showcase such graphs as a bit of braggadocio by the author, highlighting their big-time trades. (Wow! Nice. 60% gain in six months.) Here's my brag: I picked every one of these stocks, not at the beginning of the graph (lower left) but at the *end* of it (upper right). Yes, I'm bragging about picking these stocks for millions of paying customers *after* the moves you see.

And yes, I *am* bragging. Each of these stocks is among my Hall of Fame picks, rising 52 *to 1,371 times in value* from that point forward. (Apple at the low end, Amazon at the high end.)

Some pictures are worth a thousand words; these could fill a bank vault. I first wrote about this phenomenon in 1999 in *Rule Breakers, Rule Makers*, but I had to wait this long to live it, demonstrate it, and now share it. Each of these Rule Breakers, *after* the periods graphed above, obliterated the market averages, topped stock-of-the-decade lists, and carried their investors to the skies trailing clouds of glory. We now *know* this to be true; time has passed and the numbers (their volatility, too!) are real. In *every* case, these stocks exhibited:

⋯→ STELLAR PAST PRICE APPRECIATION. ←⋯

Yet, for many traders, these stocks were only thrilling short-term ventures. For others, they were an observation from the sidelines. Watching these stocks rapidly ascend and then seemingly slip away, they let them go— later recognizing these era-defining stocks as the legendary *ones that got away*, investments that might have been.

Trait #3 helps Rule Breaker investors through a hard time—the hard time of watching a stock you were interested in rise up and make a jump *without you*. It always stings a bit... until you look again at those graphs above (and many other examples), and remember: You didn't miss out. Instead you've just been given **one of my favorite signals** to lean in and finally *buy* the stock!

---

47   Side note: Love the parallels in those numbers!

Why does this work?

As mentioned in Chapter 2, did you remember to stick this phrase —"Buy high and try not to sell"—on your fridge? When you allow stellar price appreciation to guide you, you are buying high. When you buy high, you're often buying into excellence.

Why do you think that stock is hitting highs instead of new lows? Why does it keep reaching new peaks? The market likes what it sees and rewards the stock with premium pricing. You get what you pay for, as the old saying goes; that's true in the stock market, too. A world full of people who've been coached to buy low gives a great advantage to the minority of us who buy high. While others bemoan valuations and runaway stock prices, we have the privilege of buying the best companies of our time.

EVERY STOCK TRADES FOR $100 A SHARE

I hope you've already internalized Habit #2, "Add up, *don't* double down." If so, you're steps ahead in embracing stellar past price appreciation. Still, you might appreciate a couple of mental crutches to help you buy a stock you've just seen go up 60% over the previous six months.

The first is a little game I call, "Don't Look Back!" Simply put: YOU ARE NOT ALLOWED TO LOOK BACKWARD AT THE STOCK'S PRICE PERFORMANCE. Before you buy stock in a company, you may only look at the company—and its valuation, if you like (cf. Chapter 12). You're not allowed to know "it already doubled." Here's why:

1. Excellent companies do double.
2. People who notice a stock has doubled cross it off their list.
3. Excellent companies then usually double again.
4. People end up missing all the excellent companies of our time because they're looking through the rear-view mirror.

So, new game, "Don't Look Back!": You are not allowed to drive looking at the rear-view mirror. You are not allowed to invest looking at the past stock price.

Now, I know you might be thinking: *"Wait, how am I supposed to know the stock has gone up 60% if I'm not allowed to look at the stock price?"* Fair point. Yes, we can't *unsee* past performance, but the idea is not to let the past cloud your judgment in the wrong way. That a stock has shot up is not a reason to avoid it—in fact, it's a reason to *consider it further*. Excellent companies are *supposed* to rise in value. Just because they've doubled with you watching doesn't mean they're done.

So don't be discouraged by past price movements. If you would be, Don't Look Back!

There's a second mental crutch, courtesy of Peter Lynch. Lynch said, "Pretend that every stock is priced at $100 per share. Now, what do you want to own?" He used this to counter many people's instincts to favor low-priced or "penny" stocks.[48] People are attracted (too much so) to low-priced shares. They look much more attractive:

"Hey, if that 37-cent stock just goes to 75 cents, I'll double my money."

A simple question worth asking your penny-stock-loving friends: "Um, how do you think it got down to pennies in the first place?"

Meantime, many great companies and Rule Breakers have stocks priced in the triple digits. Take a look at the share price for one of the best stocks to have owned over the past 50 years, Berkshire Hathaway (trading for tens of thousands of dollars per share). Lynch's "every stock is at $100 a share" gets investors thinking more about a company's fundamentals and value, avoiding the magnet of the specific digits of the market's present price tag.[49]

This same concept can help with stellar past price appreciation. If you don't want to play my "Don't Look Back!" game, consider adopting instead the mindset that "every stock is at $100 a share," including the one you're looking at. Who cares where it was? It's at $100. *Now what do you want to own?*

---

48 These instincts seem still alive and well (and just as mistaken) today, so let's re-popularize this idea!

49 Every price per share is merely a function of how many shares of that company there are. That's part of why stock splits are overrated. When a stock split happens, say a two-for-one stock split, a company doubles its number of shares and halves its price. The value per share doesn't change; the market capitalization remains the same. The function of a share price is nothing more than how many shares the company wants to have out there for owners.

These mental crutches can help apprehensive investors buy into the face of new all-time highs for Rule Breaker stocks, an incredibly helpful step in their growth and development. Remember, **winning stocks constantly make more new highs over months and years**. That's the very definition of a winning stock; that's the shape of its graph and the pattern of its performance over time. It's "blindingly obvious," as I called O'Neil's greatest insight earlier, but only once you see it and reframe your thinking. This insight, before switching on to it, couldn't be less intuitive.

What everyone aims to do eventually, after their time of growth or recuperation, is to throw the crutches away. I encourage you to do the same. The two crutches I'm handing you are designed to help you close your eyes and hit the "buy" button on your computer or phone, *despite* the stock's stellar past price appreciation. The irony here is that stellar price appreciation isn't something to close your eyes to or rely on crutches for.

It's a feature, not a bug. It's a good thing. It's what you want to see. It's Trait #3 of the Rule Breaker stock!

DOES THIS ALWAYS WORK?

Leading off this chapter with the "months-leading-up" graphs of some of my greatest stock picks—terminating at the far right on the day that I finally picked it—illustrates a key lesson: Adopting O'Neil's mindset can yield outstanding results. But... does it always work?

I have picked so many bad stocks that were supported by this trait. Many times, after seeing a company I admired jump in stock price, I was emboldened to pick that stock... and it bombed. Please reread "Losing to Win" in Chapter 1 to understand and accept losing. If you are not okay with losing, this book may offer insights and moments of value, but I cannot fully recommend Rule Breaker Investing for you. Like venture capitalists, we lose to win. Stellar past price appreciation does not always mean you have a winning stock.

And, better news: The opposite can be true as well. The opposite of a stock that jumps, and you buy just before it bombs, is a stock that dives, and you buy just before it shoots to the moon. That does happen. Shopify, a classic Rule Breaker since the mid-2010s, was cut in half the five months before my colleague Karl Thiel picked it for Motley Fool Rule Breakers on February 24, 2016. By the end of 2024, Shopify was a 50-bagger. Part of being a Rule Breaker is breaking your own rules sometimes. Shopify had most of the earmarks of being a Rule Breaker (see Traits #1–#6, excepting #3), reminding us that not every winning stock will fit all Six Traits perfectly. The presence of as many traits as possible is stronger than none at all, and Shopify's positioning to help small businesses build online stores was peerless; I was willing to look past the cutting-in-half part.

Trait #3 still provided a win here. One month later, when it was time to make the March 2016 stock pick for Rule Breakers, I simply re-upped Shopify. This time, Shopify had stellar past price appreciation: It had jumped 30% from the previous month. Trait #3 gave me confidence to pick it a second month in a row. Now a 40-bagger, it's not quite the return of that position from a month before, but we'll take 40 times our money over eight years every time. And in a sense, we picked it with more confidence than the first time. It now had stellar past price appreciation, so: "Add up, *don't* double down."

Doug, contributing to a Motley Fool message board, articulated it well:

> Price and value are not necessarily the same thing.... A stock can have a substantial run-up, and actually be a better value at the higher price than it was at the lower price. Conversely, a stock can take a real dip in price, but not necessarily be a better value at the lower price.... It's all based on the best estimate for the future of the business at the time you purchase. It's been a difficult lesson for me to learn. (It seems sort of counterintuitive). My Scot heritage screams, 'Buy the stocks that have dropped the most since recommended... these are obviously the best values.' Not necessarily so.

NO TRAIT IN ISOLATION: A CONCERT

Some traders follow a strategy pursuing Trait #3 in isolation. They buy "momentum stocks" as "momentum players." Their watchlist is restricted to only hot stocks. (This is an oversimplification, as they'll often use price-chart patterns or other factors—some use astrology, or the movement of sea slugs!) Most momentum players are short-term even by trader standards—in it for a day, a week. The approach is antithetical to Rule Breaker Investing, but sometimes my emphasis on stellar past price appreciation can sound like momentum investing.

The key to Rule Breaker Investing is to look for our Rule Breaker Traits together, working in concert. Any one of these traits, even my favorite (Trait #1), does not stand on its own. The point of Part II is to introduce you to the key factors I've cultivated and watched win over the years. They've guided Rule Breaker investors to the top stocks of this generation. The key is, you want to see most or all of these Six Traits in place, because they work together. These traits working in concert contrasts with the Six Habits from Part I. Each of those habits stands tall on its own; it doesn't need a boost from the others to show its value. *Rule Number One: Let your winners run. High.* Full stop. *Follow the four tenets of conscious capitalism.* Full stop. Cultivate any one of those habits and you're better off.

But find and follow, in a given stock, just a single *one* of these traits? Look elsewhere.

Thus ends the first cycle of Rule Breaker stock traits; we're halfway through. The first two traits focused on the company, the third on the stock. The same sequence applies for traits #4, #5, and #6: The first two look at the company, and the third, the stock. This pattern reveals two insights: (1) as business-focused investors, we prioritize the companies themselves, but (2) ultimately, it's the stocks themselves we buy to hold. And Rule Breaker investors, when choosing stocks, are most often rewarded when we *already* see evidence of:

···→ **STELLAR PAST PRICE APPRECIATION.** ←···

CHAPTER 10

GOOD MANAGEMENT AND SMART BACKING

T HE MOTLEY FOOL launched on America Online (AOL) on August 4, 1994. Being around AOL in the early days was exciting and unbelievably educational for my brother Tom, me, and our little band of Fools. As 20-something entrepreneurs, we learned lifelong lessons, from adapting to new technology (the internet), to working with a big partner (AOL, not always easy), making payroll, building a brand, and doing media appearances with our jester caps on. We met and did business with Jeff Bezos of Amazon, Meg Whitman of eBay, Jerry Yang at Yahoo!, and Howard Schultz of Starbucks, and others whose names were quicker lost to history.

Getting to know many of the best (and some of the worst) people in business provided a priceless education[50] for me, who started out as an armchair investor. I'd been raised to keep my eyes on market headlines, my nose in Value Line (the old black-bindered, thin-papered investment research service), and my fingers tapping away at spreadsheets, tracking ratios and metrics.

---

50   Priceless. But even better: Free!

For me growing up (and for many still today), investing was mainly a math exercise, focused on estimating growth rates, looking at valuation multiples, projecting target prices and rates of return. *Math.* What else did one have to go on but one's own scribblings? We had no access to today's voluminous and free real-time data. Research back then involved obtaining the telephone number of a company's investor relations department (a research task in itself) to make a toll-free (or not) phone call to request a paper copy of a company's most recent annual report or 10-K. This kind of investment research is *far* removed from the businesses themselves, which were almost curios, untouchable to the investor, and thus abstracted from tangible reality.

That had been then, but this was now: By dint of our entrepreneurial enterprise, we young investors now had a front-row seat looking into the real workings of the businesses we'd once *researched*, the real lives and conversations of those regularly featured in business headlines.

The prominent figure we got to know best was Steve Case, the brilliant founder and CEO of America Online in its golden age, the 1990s... the decade America went online. The price of going online back then was astronomical compared to today. Early adopters paid *hourly* connection fees to dial up AOL's servers over their phone lines using 2400 baud modems (making *that screeching sound*); AOL charged a few bucks an hour to increasing numbers of people discovering the merit and possibilities of the new medium. Years later, the cost of coming online would move to a flat fee and flatten much of AOL along with it. But not so, back then. AOL was the top dog and first-mover and had pricing power— and at one key point, AOL *raised* its rates.

The day the news came out, I was at a corporate offsite conference for AOL partners. That evening, with cocktail in hand, I sidled up to Steve because I wanted to hear his take. All day I'd been seeing headlines from *The New York Times, Wall Street Journal,* CNBC, and their ilk: "AOL makes a horrible decision, it's raising rates." In contrast to the uncertainty and drama in the headlines, Case calmly and confidently let these rhetorical questions sit in the evening air: "Don't you think we've already market-tested this for the last six months or so? Don't you think we already know exactly what's going to happen with these numbers? Do you really think this is a bad decision we're making?"

Again, this was the early days of AOL and the Fool, and that night left a lasting impression. I had picked the stock, months before, as a true-blue Rule Breaker (though I wouldn't have used that language then). The pre-Motley Fool investor in me would only have seen that day's lurid headlines. But now, the businessman in me had access to the entrepreneur himself, leaving those words in the night air. Other members of his team—our business operational partners—were people I respected. *Pace* Bethany McLean's and Peter Elkind's 2003 book, these were "the smartest guys in the room" at that point in online history. They stood on one side, while on the other were journalists and pundits (often backed by advertisers competing with America Online...).

That price hike ended up being a great move for AOL; consumers didn't blink, and its premium pricing gave AOL big cash flows that accelerated its growth rates, and left competition in the dust. As the company merged with Time Warner in 2000, the stock price from my cost basis *had risen 150 times in value*. I had my first 100-bagger.

I now knew something really important that I hadn't even known when I'd first recommended the stock. I could see that what mattered much more than pundits, hot takes, and news cycles—and yes, even my own spreadsheet math—was:

⋯⟶ GOOD MANAGEMENT AND SMART BACKING. ⟵⋯

Contrasting the bullish assertions of the lone CEO with the bearish megaphone of the national media—and *then* seeing how the business and the stock *actually* played out—told me what I needed to know. Eye-opener.

"PERSON OF THE YEAR"

My favorite Warren Buffett line sums up this learning perfectly:

> I'm a better investor because I'm a businessman, and a better businessman because I'm an investor.

Buffett excels at both, showing how each role enhances the other. Insights from one role (your *yin*) naturally inform the other (your *yang*). I envision a rising vortex where each pushes the other upward, continually reaching higher, *excelsior*.

No one exemplifies this better than Buffett. It's why I urge talented business friends to do their own investing, and investing friends to spend more time in real businesses (especially those on the cutting edge, with faster growth rates and greater adoption of new technology). **The better you get at one, the better you'll become at the other.** *Denying* yourself the experience of either will reduce your growth in the other.

Getting Things Done author David Allen says, "The better you get, the better you'd *better* get," reminding us that winning requires a lifelong commitment to curiosity. Another favorite of mine, which I first heard attributed to Archbishop William Temple: "The greater the island of knowledge, the longer the coastline of mystery."

It is this human dynamic that drives Trait #4. After showcasing stellar past price appreciation, Trait #4 reminds us that behind every stock is a business, and behind every business are the people who conceived, birthed, and run it. *People*, more so than products or technologies or next quarter's earnings (or your spreadsheet), are the most important driver of future growth. Your research hours should focus on the character and genius of the people running the enterprise. Remember Schopenhauer's quote from Chapter 7:

> Talent hits a target no one else can hit.
> Genius hits a target no one else can see.

Geniuses are out there in every industry, often founding and running Rule Breaker companies. Pick the stocks with the geniuses running them, because recognizing and respecting human character will hugely affect your returns as an investor.

It is no coincidence that Rule Breaker CEOs often wind up Business Person of the Year (but always years after the stock has skyrocketed). Reed Hastings won Business Person of the Year from *Fortune* in 2010, six years after I'd recommended the stock. Jeff Bezos was *Time*'s Person of the Year in 1999, two years after I picked the stock.[51] Tesla was my November 2011 Rule Breakers stock pick, and 10 years later Elon Musk was named *Time*'s Person of the Year. Nvidia founder Jensen Huang was *Fortune*'s Business Person of the Year in 2017, 12 years after I started holding the stock. They've all done well since.

Turns out one of the best indicators of the great stocks of a generation are the CEOs and founders who end up being "Person of the Year." It's a great buy indicator if only you could have known ahead of time, right? But you can. Do what I do: *Look at the humans*, when everyone else focuses on financial ratios, technical indicators, or analyst forecasts. Today's investors have unprecedented access to corporate leaders' thoughts via social media, press interviews, YouTube, LinkedIn, and conference presentations. Look for:

··⟶ *GOOD MANAGEMENT AND SMART BACKING.* ⟵··

ARE YOU A GOOD JUDGE OF CHARACTER?

Some readers will have cocked an eye at this point, looking askance, wondering, how can we actually know who's a genius and who's not, who's a good person, and who's not? I'm making it sound too easy.

Since you're reading this book, you're ahead of the game. You're

---

51   Much quicker than usual. Give the journalists their due.

discerning already! You value honesty, the power of purpose, you look for servant leaders. More importantly, especially in emergent Rule Breakers, you seek visionaries. Steve Jobs may not have been easy to work with, but we esteem his otherworldly vision, his passion, care, and commitment. The traits we admire in our heroes are what you look for in the people you're investing in. I'm a fan of leaders with a sense of humor. (I also believe the winners of most democratic contests are those more voters would want to shoot pool with.) Sometimes I'm right, sometimes wrong. Most of us get better at judging character over time; it's called wisdom. Asking this question and caring about it, in the context of investment research, already makes you a Rule Breaker.

But here are a couple more thoughts. First, when deciding whether the CEO or founders are for real, *tie goes to saying yes.* If we're talking about Rule Breaker or potential Rule Breaker companies, these are people who have steered their enterprise into being the top dog and first-mover in an important, emerging industry; from the proverbial garage, they have taken their companies public and demonstrated sustainable advantage; their stocks have outstandingly appreciated. Give 'em the benefit of the doubt! (Of course, if you have strong negative feelings, just find other companies.)

Second, many great Rule Breaker founders and CEOs have what I call "a lover's quarrel" with their industries.[52] They started a company because they had a better solution than the status quo, than what the Rule Makers offer. These leaders know their industry inside and out, they *love* it, but they recognize its problems. They have a vision and a passion for fixing those problems with lower prices, more accessibility or ease of use, new technologies. They are not just the smartest people in the room for their industry (usually they are); they have more heart than their competitors, too. And that's why so many of our Rule Breakers wind up having their founders named Person of the Year a decade hence. It's not really that hard to see. You just have to look and care.

---

52 The line "I had a lover's quarrel with the world," from Robert Frost's poem "The Lesson for Today," adorns Frost's gravestone.

In fact, I have a lover's quarrel with how people invest. That's what helped give rise to The Motley Fool. It's why I wrote this book.

One of my heroes, *Wired* co-founder Kevin Kelly, points to another trait I highly esteem: an abundance mentality.[53] In his book *Excellent Advice for Living*, he writes:

Go with the option that opens up yet more options.

This counters the common advice about focus, where success is seen as a product of ruthless self-denial, spartan simplification—choosing *only* one thing, never two or four.

Kelly advises favoring choices that unlock new possibilities; similarly, I favor CEOs who constantly create more options for their businesses. I seek *optionality* as a key attribute of my favorite stocks, and it's present in companies like Amazon or Nvidia. Rocking my inner Kelly: **Go with the business that is opening up yet more options for itself.**

Jeff Bezos exemplifies this. Amazon started as an online bookseller but now has infinite options. Leaders with a growth mindset and an abundance mentality,[54] who go with the option that opens up yet more options, are my kind of CEOs. Your mileage may vary.

The key lies in continually asking these questions and refining your evaluations. You'll improve with practice. Remember, all Six Traits are designed to operate *in concert*; this one is not a standalone litmus test.

UM... WHAT ABOUT THE "BACKING" PART?

The major points have been made, and they're all about the leaders and founders, the culture they create, their genius and vision, or lack thereof. That seems concentrated on the good management part, but the language

---

53   This relates as well to the work of Carol Dweck, which favors growth mindsets over those that are fixed.

54   I often contrast the abundance mentality with its ugly step-cousin, the tradeoff mentality, exhibited by people who focus on scarcity and zero-sum thinking, believing that gaining one thing always means losing another.

of Trait #4 gives equal weight to "smart backing."

Backing refers to the people who finance these emerging companies: the angel investors, venture capitalists, the backers. They matter too. Just as you can find lots of professional and personal information about CEOs today, you can find just as much on the backers. It's worth looking at, because the quality (or lack thereof) of investors in Rule Breaker enterprises is meaningful and telling. For example, firms like Kleiner Perkins and Andreesen Horowitz have built recognizable brands that give you a sense of the pedigree of the companies they invest in.

However, as public market investors, we're not quite as concerned about the institutional monies that started out in these companies, or even for the most part who is invested in them today. Certainly, who is invested in companies is not as important as who is running them. Often, they're the same; that's my way of saying we should favor companies where the CEO (especially founding CEOs) owns a lot of their stock, where the backers are the leaders.

Backing does matter, but not as much to me today as when I wrote the chapter on this topic in *Rule Breakers, Rule Makers*. These days, I still include backing alongside management, and they both count. However, I now place far more weight on the founders and leadership. So while I might be giving a bit of lip service to backers here, lip service is still service. But they're not equally weighted.

One exception. I often find the best backers to be extremely articulate and insightful in their writings and speeches. We picture CEOs mostly running their companies; backers, on the other hand, run their mouths— they build their reputations by sharing their intellect and insights. It's how they get the attention of the best entrepreneurs of the future; they court them, in part, through their expressions. (The backer's own past record of backing matters most of all, of course!)

A good example is the team that formed and led Y Combinator, the American firm that accelerates start-ups. Sam Altman of OpenAI fame was a higher-up, and co-founder Paul Graham has written many pieces of interest to Rule Breaker investors.[55] Bill Gurley at Benchmark is another sterling example. There are others. Oh, for instance, what about Warren Buffett? He's a backer, and a constant commentator for decades on what he thinks works in investing!

So backers, and their reputations, count for something too.

Rule Breaker investors are *business-focused* investors. Part of caring about the businesses in which you invest—their purpose, products, cultures, and competitive strengths—is what underpins them all: their people. A great Rule Breaker investor is competent in evaluating the human dynamic. And it's worth repeating that if you're barking up this tree, know that comparatively few others are. And that is greatly to our advantage. Fools run contrary to conventional wisdom. That's why we esteem and insist on:

··→ GOOD MANAGEMENT AND SMART BACKING. ←··

---

55 Here's a good one: Paul Graham, "Black Swan Farming," paulgraham.com/swan.html (September 2012).

CHAPTER 11

STRONG CONSUMER APPEAL

"Win the crowd, and you will win your freedom."
—PROXIMO (FROM THE MOVIE *GLADIATOR*)

NATURAL SELECTION DOESN'T just govern biology—it drives business, too.

Businesses compete to serve customers, who will naturally select the products and services they prefer. The dollars spent by those customers fuel the firms they buy from, enabling those companies to thrive, giving them the resources necessary to flourish and propagate. Winning businesses are thus enabled to pass on their *genes* (their business models, their balance sheets, their customer bases, their cultures) to the next era—to keep doing business for another generation.

The more I observe what actually wins in the marketplace, the more I respect the power of brands. Thinking of Proximo's famous line from *Gladiator*, in the arena of business, brands that resonate deeply, create loyalty, and stand for something customers can't live without are the brands that win the crowd. Strong brands don't just score one-off victories. They deliver every day on the promises that they make, from their marketing claims, to their product quality, to the trust they hope to build with every interaction.

I like Proximo's line for its second clause, as well. He reminds us as stakeholders—whether as entrepreneurial founders, as employees, or even merely (here) as investors in great brands—winning the crowd in business does indeed grant freedom—financial freedom! When Rule Breakers win the crowd, they can win your freedom. They've won mine, over and over.

In their book *The Why of Work*, authors Dave and Wendy Ulrich define brand compellingly: "A company brand presents a point of view about the company, proposes a lifestyle consistent with that point of view, and shapes customer expectations."

This view of brands goes well beyond a superficial view of them as "brand names" with "name recognition" that influence snap choices made in grocery aisles. The Ulrichs say that the best brands—through an eldritch mix of product effectiveness, price, appearance, a dollop of storytelling, and maybe a unicorn's hair or two—ultimately propose lifestyles, and consistently enable their customers to live out those lifestyles.

A look at the world's most valuable brands in 2024 as compiled by Brand Finance shows many examples. Top 10 brands like Apple, Amazon, Walmart, Facebook (Instagram, etc.), and TikTok are valued by their customers far beyond the cost of their products or services. That many of the most valuable brands are also some of the world's most valuable companies tells you what you need to know. Rule Breaker investors should be looking for:

···**→** **STRONG CONSUMER APPEAL.** **←**···

WHAT TOOTHPASTE TEACHES

We live in an attention-starved world. In their insightful 2000 book *Simplicity Marketing*, authors Steven Cristol and Peter Sealey point out what's happened to toothpaste. Back in the day, there were a few brands to choose from at your local pharmacy: Crest, Colgate, a few others. Today, just Crest alone fills the pharmacy aisle with dozens of versions, leading to what Alvin Toffler called "overchoice." Do you want the toothpaste tube or pump? Gel? Liquid? Tartar control? Cavity Protection, or would you prefer 3D Advanced? Complete Whitening (Plus Scope)? Baking Soda & Peroxide?

Gum Detoxify?

And this is just toothpaste!

Multiply the number of different products you need to pick up at the grocery store, times the number of different brands, times the number of variations *within* a brand (we hadn't yet talked about Crest Whitening Strips—did you want to pick up some of those?), and the total boggles the mind.

That's why Cristol and Sealey wisely champion the ability of great brands to cut through the noise and make our lives simpler. You had a good experience with that product or service? You remember the brand? (Maybe it was even a bit catchy?) In our increasingly complex world swarming with overchoice, brand loyalties enable us to simplify our decision-making and choose with confidence.

Brands that enable customers to replace multiple brands with one brand, or multiple choices with one choice, create exceptional (and often unrecognized) value. Walmart's big-box stores replaced many errand stops. Amazon did the same, but one-upped them by eliminating the need to go out at all. Then, Amazon replaced many brands with its own "Amazon" brand. I used to care about battery brands; now I just buy "Amazon Basics" batteries (delivered by an Amazon truck). Amazon private label products stretch from electronics to home goods to office supplies and more. One can even further simplify and subscribe to recurring shipments.

No wonder Amazon's brand is the fourth most valuable in the world! Just seeing the names "Amazon," "Starbucks," "Disney," "Uber," or "J.P. Morgan" is enough for many to click, transact, travel, or deposit money with confidence and trust. Especially with overchoice, complexity, new technologies, and general overwhelm, these companies have incredible consumer appeal.[56]

---

56 Note that there are haters out there too for every one of the world's biggest brands, which itself is actually a good sign; people care.

But here I am lionizing the ones who have *made* it. Big deal, right? Sure, Apple: huge brand, huge market cap. "Tell me something I don't know," you may be saying.

Okay, here's something most people don't know: You can and should actively be using Trait #5 to find the world's *next* great brands, many of which will also become the world's next great stocks. Since the mid-1990s, I've been seeking great brands and brand builders, knowing their value will show up in stock performance, *even if not in financial statements.*

ATTRIBUTES OF WINNING BRANDS

I'll speak to that latter point in a minute, but first let me offer some tips on brand-spotting.

Looking at the world's great brands (including many Rule Breaker stocks I picked when imagining them as future top 100 brands seemed laughable), we can identify a short but growing list of attributes. Here are things I see and look for (with a few exemplars):

Bright: Great brands use language and imagery that is bright, inspiring, wholesome, and/or aspirational. You'll find few "dark" and "edgy" examples among the corporate greats (Disney, LEGO, Southwest Airlines).

Responsible: In line with Habit #4 (follow the four tenets of conscious capitalism), great brands pursue great purposes, demonstrate responsibility, and make that responsibility transparent to customers and competitors alike (Nike, Patagonia, Tesla).

Affectionate: Great brands put customers first, design with empathy, create emotional connections (Amazon, Apple, Warby Parker).

Notable: It's the same memorable tagline, the same melodic jingle, every time (Intel, McDonald's, State Farm).

Dependable: Same cup of coffee, every time, too (IKEA, Starbucks, Zoom Video).

I bet you can come up with more attributes and your own favorite examples. (Though if you do, you may mess up my elegant B-R-A-N-D mnemonic!) My purpose here is not to provide an exhaustive analysis. Similar to Chapter 8 where we looked at Sustainable Competitive Advantage, whole books are worthy of your attention should you wish to deepen your knowledge on this topic.[57] Brand sleuths can also follow studies like Interbrand's Best Global Brands or lists like *Fortune*'s Most Admired or Fast Company's Most Innovative.

The key takeaway here is to notice and to care. For any company you're researching, is its brand valued by its buyers? Does it have raving fans?[58] Most of us think in terms of consumer brands, but businesses that sell successfully to other businesses succeed in part because they exhibit similarly strong appeal. Consumer appeal, like great cities, is built over time and becomes a powerful asset.

But there I go again, mentioning ("asset") a term from financial statements! Which brings me to a very special reason to appreciate brand....

HIDDEN IN PLAIN SIGHT

Strong consumer appeal has been a bedrock of Rule Breaker Investing since I first included it among my Six Traits back in 1999. It's guided me to pick many Rule Breakers—stocks that have gone on to win the crowd (and financial freedom for many Motley Fool members). Even an upstart like Nvidia, with its consumer-*un*friendly name[59]—nowhere *near* the list of top brands back in 2005—was (19 years later) in 2024 picked as the world's fastest-growing. The ties between winning brands and winning stocks run deep, and both ways.

But the best reason of all that Rule Breaker investors should seek out brand and consumer appeal is that they are not accounted for in any

---

57 Some of my favorites that speak to branding and consumer appeal: *Brand Hijack* by Alex Wipperfürth; *Creativity Inc.* by Ed Catmull; *It's Not What You Sell It's What You Stand For* by Roy Spence; *Made to Stick* by Chip & Dan Heath; *Setting the Table* by Danny Meyer; *Youtility* by Jay Baer; and anything and everything by Seth Godin (*Purple Cow* etc.).

58 *Will it pass your own Henrik's T-shirt Test?* Ah, but that comes up in Chapter 13....

59 Many people continue to mispronounce it as "Nuh-vidia"—it's the most mispronounced global top brand.

consistent, meaningful, or evident way in financial statements. That's because a brand is considered an "intangible asset," not something like cash, inventory, or property that is clearly visible and quantifiable on the balance sheet. Hardcore bean-counting accountants[60] are unwilling to put real numbers on the connection and trust built between a company and its customers. Customer delight, belonging, authenticity, nostalgia, and *satisfaction* in the relationship that exists between sellers and buyers cannot be captured or recognized in financial statements.

Which means that **brand, one of the most critical and valuable components of lasting business dominance, is "hidden in plain sight."**

You and I can *plainly* see it, know it. Esteem it! But investors relying on traditional valuation work do not. Most use multiples (price-to-earnings, price-to-cash-flow, price-to-book—sometimes dividend yields). To them and their enterprise values (EBITDA, EV/sales), strong consumer appeal is utterly missing. Thus, with their denominators not accounting for the ultimate soft-skill of entrepreneurship—brand-building—they skip the Rule Breakers: "Overvalued," they say, sometimes with an eye-roll. And so they fail to buy the stocks of the Rule Breakers, the companies being "naturally selected" *en masse*, the ones that will pass on their genes to the next generation.[61] It simply doesn't register for them:

··→ STRONG CONSUMER APPEAL. ←··

Trait #5 is not the only one we look for in Rule Breaker stocks; remember, as conveyed earlier, these six instruments play together in concert.

Oh... and it's not the only key attribute "hidden in plain sight," either.

The secret sauce of Rule Breaker Investing resides in the next chapter.

---

60 Some of my best friends are accountants.

61 This may also be why many of them don't hold what they buy for long. They're not buying the ones worth holding.

CHAPTER 12

"OVERVALUED"

"Hello, world."

—TIGER WOODS

RAIT #6 MAKES no sense. It should be the opposite...!

...especially when paired with Trait #3 (stellar past price appreciation, from Chapter 9). It's the ultimate Rule Breaker sequence: (1) we want to see the stock rise significantly *before* we buy, and (2) then we want to hear from professional financial commentators that the stock is overpriced, overhyped.

What I just wrote is crazy. Could these be more contrarian? From the earliest age bouncing on their mama's knee, little investors are taught that (1) you want to find a stock that is beaten down and near its 52-week low, and (2) you want experts validating your decision with "strong buy" ratings.

And maybe that really does work; I'm not speaking to what may or may not work for others. This book features what has worked for me, and that is: looking in the short term like a rube, overpaying for overvalued stocks my whole career.

Remember how badly Nike "overpaid" for Tiger Woods? The year was 1996, and Tiger was just 20 years old, with not a single PGA tournament win under his belt. He signed an endorsement deal for a staggering *$40 million* with Nike—equivalent to $80 million today when adjusted for inflation. At the time, this seemed outrageous. How could a kid who had never raised a trophy as a pro get so much hype—and so much money?! (What do you think his price-to-PGA-earnings ratio was?) To put it in perspective, $40 million was unheard of for a golfer back then. A decade before, NBA rookie Michael Jordan had signed his first Nike contract for $2.5 million over five years. Almost gets your dander up all over again now, eh?

If so, you may not be a Rule Breaker investor.

Because in that story—which wound up being a brilliant investment for Nike—two key elements were at play. First, Tiger exhibited **stellar past price appreciation**. He hadn't made any money yet, but the week before his pro debut he won the U.S. amateur championship... for the third time. Days later, *The New York Times* speculated he would turn pro the following weekend at the Greater Milwaukee Open, which then swarmed with 150,000 spectators (its largest-ever draw). Sure enough, Tiger entered that tournament as a professional and opened his first-round press conference with, "Hello, world."[62] Second, many in the industry questioned whether a relatively unknown young golfer could justify such a large investment. "Show me!" the skeptics crowed. Or in investment parlance: **"Overvalued."**

Why did signing Tiger work? Why has Intuitive Surgical (ISRG) worked? In the five months before I picked it in March 2005, against a sideways market, the company's stock had risen 75%. The day I picked it, the stock traded at 71 times its earnings per share. Stellar past price appreciation. Overvalued.

Why signing Tiger worked is why Intuitive Surgical worked: *Because they are great.*

Tiger went on to be *Sports Illustrated*'s Sportsman of the Year for 1996 and racked up 82 PGA tournament wins, tied for #1 all time with Sam Snead. Intuitive Surgical has parlayed its "Snap Cola" positioning, being the only one doing minimally invasive robotic-driven surgery at scale for decades now, and as I was writing this book crossed over into

---

62   This wasn't spontaneous, but carefully choreographed with Nike launching the "Hello World" campaign days later. He finished that first tournament in 60th place, by the way, good enough for $2,544.

100-bagger territory, hitting the 100-bagger gong for me on the final day of August 2024.[63]

Pulling a line from Chapter 7: I try to find excellence, buy excellence, and add to excellence over time. I sell mediocrity. That's how I invest.

So yes, absolutely: Rule Breaker Investing has us looking for the greatest companies in the world. Full stop. There are at least three reasons why this works:

1. If you invest for greatness, you'll be way ahead of the game. Most people don't recognize greatness initially (or impugn it). They need others and the media to call it great first—*so you bought before they did.*

2. If you invest for greatness, you'll be way ahead of the envy crowd. Some smart people recognize greatness but are envious. They may see the greatness, but green-eyed, they will talk it down and scare others away—*so you bought before they did.*

3. If you invest for greatness, you will show fortitude through the inevitable slumps (like Tiger's) or significant sell-offs (ISRG had five 33%+ sell-offs over 20 years)—*so you sell after they did.*

As you can see, investing for greatness means the stocks will look hot (Trait #3) and be priced expensively (Trait #6), which keeps many investors away while we establish our positions. Traits #3 and #6 are interlinked: They focus solely on the stock. The other four traits focus on the company itself, which is what matters most. But Traits #3 and #6 are the picture frame, and you want the frame to fit the picture. That's why I emphasize these traits working together. And the one that *completes* the picture is the commonly held perception, especially when validated by financial headlines or TV pronouncements, that the stock is:

··→ **"OVERVALUED."** ←··

---

63   In the first draft of this chapter, it had been up 82 times in value—*82*—same number as Tiger's PGA wins. Kismet! So yeah, the irony of an 82-bagger would have been elegant, but we'll just accept the 100+-bagger instead.

It's the cherry on top.

THERE ARE NO NUMBERS
FOR THE THINGS THAT MATTER MOST

I've thought for a long time about why this works. *That* it works is beyond question. Several decades of investing results through many environments have shown me all I need to see. But why these Six Traits work together, especially Trait #6, has been an ongoing fascination.

While this is not a single-variable problem, I like to reduce things to their simplest explanations; as Einstein is widely credited with saying, "Everything should be made as simple as possible, but not simpler."[64] Here's my best effort at explaining what's going on.

It started last chapter when I pointed out that brand is not traditionally measurable on financial statements, so most valuation work doesn't acknowledge it. Stocks are broadly perceived to be valued on their earnings or cash flow; the company's share price and market cap are viewed as multiples of these things only. Thus, companies with valuable brands always look overvalued because one of their best traits is counted for naught! That's the beginning of this basic "overvalued" dynamic.

But brand isn't the only value ignored by so many investors. Not even close. Additional examples abound of things not measured by traditional valuation work, and—your High Irony alarm sirens should be going off about now!—they are many of the things that matter *most*. Earnings and cash flow are outputs, not inputs. They are outcomes. I'm trying to help my Rule Breaker Investor padawans see the factors that underlie and generate those outputs. That's what we're looking at. And for many of these things—just like strong consumer appeal, but by no means limited to it: There are no numbers for the things that matter most.

Do any come to mind for you?

How about the CEO? Do you think the founders and leaders of businesses—especially emergent ones, especially potential Rule Breakers—

---

64 He never actually said it. Check it. (Ironically, he said something much more complicated, that has been simplified to this version!)

matter a lot to the enterprise? We already talked about that: For many of my best stock picks, years later the CEO was declared "Person of the Year." That really matters.

"We have Jeff Bezos. You don't."

"We have Elon Musk. You don't."

"We have Jensen Huang. You don't."

These are ready examples that anyone can appreciate, but of course I see the same dynamic with lesser-known CEOs of younger-stage companies like Jeff Green at The Trade Desk, Marcos Galperin at MercadoLibre, and Tobi Lütke at Shopify.

The opposite is also true. *There are value-destroying leaders in place at companies large and small today.*

So where's the line on the financial statements to adjust our esteem of a company based on its leader(s)? Right. They don't teach that in accounting school. It's counted for naught.

Brand... leadership... what else?

How about culture? I know a thing or two (not much more than that)[65] about company culture, enough to recognize that it is integral to the success or failure of companies, Rule Breakers included. Culture can be more important than leadership; leadership can change in an instant, but culture is built over time. We deeply respect and study the cultures built up in our cities and ancient civilizations... yet to many market analysts, evaluating the culture of company workplaces sounds like la-la land.

As stockpickers and investors, we ignore workplace cultures to our detriment. One can plausibly argue that Culture (capitalized, writ large) trumps Leadership *and* Brand in importance. To business author and thinker Peter Drucker, it even trumped corporate strategy: "Culture eats strategy for breakfast."[66] And yet it, too, is counted for naught.

One more example: Innovation, otherwise known as a company's

---

65 In 2014 and then again in 2015, The Motley Fool has twice been named by Glassdoor as "The #1 Small-to-Medium-Sized Company To Work For." This is a tribute to our leadership team and the 400+ employees (many of them 10+ years with us) who breathe life into our workplace every day.

66 He never actually said it. Check it. But the sentiment does succinctly summarize his beliefs.

ability to think its way out of a paper bag. "Think" doesn't capture the half of it. As Seth Godin writes in *Free Prize Inside*, great ideas are everywhere. What's truly needed, and far more valuable, are the people who'll design, develop, and deploy great ideas into the real world. Innovation is vital to Rule Breaker success over the long term, underpinning many traits: Innovators *are top dogs and first-movers*, innovation forms the basis of their *sustainable competitive advantage*, and it becomes integral to their *brands* and consumer expectations.

My stock-picking advice boils down to this:[67] "Seek out the innovators in every industry." That stocked pond is where you want your fishing line.

But is there a number that accurately conveys the value of Innovation on financial statements?

Almost! In contrast to Brand and Leadership and Culture, there are some numbers that serve as proxies, like research and development expenditures (R&D) as a percentage of revenues. In 2023, Intuitive Surgical spent $999 million on R&D, 16% of revenues. Apple spent $29.9 billion on R&D, 8% of its revenues. These numbers alone don't tell us much. Apple spends more, but is way bigger. Intuitive spends 30 times less, but more as a percentage of revenues. Both are innovators in their industries.

So even where numbers are available, we can't do much with them. Sure, we can compare companies in the same industry, but is one company's R&D dollar equivalent to another's? In 2007, the year the iPhone came out, Nokia spent $7.7 billion on R&D (12% of its revenues). Apple spent $782 million on R&D, almost exactly *one-tenth* of what Nokia spent. The rest is history: Nokia stock has gone from $35 to $4 since 2008. Even when numbers are available, they can mislead. (Numbers usually give extra confidence to those using them.)

And thus, the supposed "business intangibles," rooted in the "soft skills" of business (inputs, not outcomes), are counted for naught. Yet they provide the essential electricity powering businesses to greatness or to mediocrity! Brand, Leadership, Culture, and Innovation are especially

---

67 Did you really need to buy and read this whole book?

present in every generation's Rule Breakers. They create these companies' "hard blue glow" of greatness.[68]

There are no numbers for the things that matter most.

I see this most clearly and feel this most acutely because I have literally watched the company I co-founded grow from a paper newsletter to a billion-dollar enterprise. Instead of only researching other people's companies, I have had the privilege (and heartbreak, and glory) of watching a tiny Foolish acorn grow to an oak. I would never ignore or underrate Brand, Leadership, Culture, and Innovation.

Yet our traditional-to-modern ways of valuing stocks do ignore and underrate these things. Entirely. After decades of inquiry, I've concluded that investment analysis often arrives at the opposite conclusions in the case of Rule Breaker stocks.[69]

In the musical (and now smash-hit movie) *Wicked*, "It's all about Popular," Glinda sings. In the book *Rule Breaker Investing*, it's all about:

···→ *"OVERVALUED."* ←···

SO... UM... WHAT ARE WE SUPPOSED TO *DO*?

To some—you?—the conclusion just reached will be disconcerting. The natural inclination would be to turn to the author, as kings and queens once turned to their counselors, and demand: "What are you going to do about this? Give me an answer, author man."

Ah, but your author in this case is a Fool, which means my first inclination is to point out these ironies, as we look together at the state of today's investing conventional wisdom. And also to raise a smile! Isn't

---

68 Hat tip to John Updike, whose essay detailing the last at-bat of Ted Williams's career, *Hub Fans Bid Kid Adieu*, is indelibly etched in my memory, including that his greatness imbued him with a "hard blue glow."

69 In *Why The Bottom Line Isn't*, authors Ulrich and Smallwood summarize research suggesting that 50% of the market value of public companies is attributable to intangibles.

that why kings and queens have always needed, in some cases loved, their Fools?

That may come across smugly, or too clever by half. If the things that matter most really do matter, I should probably be inventing numbers for them, right? But I'm not. So then how are *you* supposed to do so, you may be wondering? Many will feel ill-equipped for the task... while a few others will likely roll up their sleeves, invent some valuable new toys, and become famous a generation hence. So we can look forward to the new better R&D figures a visionary accountant may one day suggest (some existing measures like ROII—return on innovation investment—go some way up this tree), as well as perhaps some new Leadership Quotient, Brand Total Value Add, and Culture Thermometer.[70]

Lacking those, the real point here is that the Six Traits of the Rule Breaker Stock give you what you need to know, without always supplying numbers. That's part of the point. Remember that most professionals and pundits are leading with, and leaning hard on, their numbers. And so when there are no numbers for the things that matter most, they are, all of them, misled. This makes "Overvalued" work!

Most investment analysts frame investing decisions as math decisions. If *no* one were, I would be! But when everyone is, rewards accrue for not doing so. The reasoning, and especially the market-beating results, should be evident. Most analysts pursue "valuation" as their justification for buy/sell decisions. But what if you assume, as I have, that there is no particular edge to be gained by valuation-centered work?

What if you shed that assumption?

---

70 They have to be working acronyms, right? For now, respectively, let's go with: For leadership, Best Organizational Stewardship Score (B.O.S.S.); for brand, Brand Leverage In Net Gains (B.L.I.N.G.); and for culture, Cultural Health Indicator of Leadership and Loyalty (C.H.I.L.L.).

THE MARKET LOOKS SIX MONTHS AHEAD

In his classic *The Structure of Scientific Revolutions*, author Thomas S. Kuhn introduced paradigm shifts in science, where established assumptions are challenged, leading to breakthroughs. Shedding old assumptions is crucial for progress.

For years, I've shed the assumption that intense valuation work is necessary. I'm generally an "EMT" proponent, leaning toward The Efficient Market Theory and its assumption that financial markets are "informationally efficient," reflecting all available information at any given time...

... ASTERISK: I think the market only looks six months ahead.

The prices you see aren't "insane" or highly undervalued or overvalued. If they were, buyers or sellers would swoop in and quickly[71] correct the mispricing. Sorry, Virginia, there is no edge based on your discounted cash-flow work or your determination that today's price-to-earnings ratio is "wrong."

Let's dive deeper. Efficient pricing in the near term prevents meaningful valuation-driven insights *looking six months ahead*. For investors who look three years out or more, you're looking at least six times further out than the market! That's our edge as business-focused investors. We find great businesses, which will trade at premiums (the best of anything usually does), and own them through timeframes that boggle Wall Street institutional minds. We prosper greatly (and work less hard).

I've always liked six months as my benchmark. First, it feels right (like Aristotle's Golden Mean), and second, it's two quarters forward. With much of the world asking, "What are earnings going to be next quarter?"[72] it may be a stretch to say the market looks two quarters ahead. But I think the market is smarter than these "next quarter" investors, so I credit it with looking one further quarter out.

---

71   Instantaneously, in this era of algorithmic trades made inside of a second.

72   And, "Will the stock pop?!!"

Imagine, then, my delight when I found this posting on Twitter/X by my friend and long-time fellow Fool, Joe Magyer:

Joe Magyer ✔ @Magyer · May 20, 2021 ···
The median professional portfolio manager invests with a time horizon of only 6 months. Hard to believe but true.

What best describes your investment time horizon at this moment?

3 months or less	47
6 months	62
9 months	24
12 months or more	55
Weighted average	**7.4**
Don't know	6

Source: BofA Global Fund Manager Survey

Mic drop.

As a long-term stockholder, the valuation at which one bought long ago ("71 times Intuitive Surgical's earnings") was indicative of only a near-term reality that real-world business results would soon render inconsequential.

So, think about it: We're not just shedding the assumption that valuation-centered work will lead to better decision-making. I'm making a new assumption: That discovering a stock widely perceived as overvalued is worth considering as the ultimate confirmation of a Rule Breaker *buy* signal.

Heretical, I know.

Except that scientific, technological, medical, business, and (yes) investing lore is full of examples of heretics disrupting the status quo and winning, creating something better.

Within our investing context, this was well understood (irony alert, again) by someone whom many observers today credit as the ultimate exemplar upholding the *importance* of valuation work:

In general, no. I am no longer an advocate of elaborate techniques of security analysis in order to find superior value opportunities. This was a rewarding activity, say, 40 years ago, when our textbook 'Graham and Dodd' was first published; but the situation has changed a great deal since then. In the old days, any well-trained security analyst could do a good professional job of selecting undervalued issues through detailed studies; but in the light of the enormous amount of research now being carried on, I doubt whether in most cases such extensive efforts will generate sufficiently superior selections to justify their cost. To that very limited extent I'm on the side of the 'efficient market' school of thought now generally accepted by the professors.

Benjamin Graham, 1976

HINDSIGHT WILL ALWAYS BE 20/20

'Tis a curious thing, that label "overvalued." At first, it's the pundits' way of warning you off—a signal from the so-called experts to stay far away from stocks like Amazon, Tesla, Intuitive Surgical, and Apple. You've heard it before: "Too expensive, too risky." Better wait for the dip....

Except the stock just keeps rising, and suddenly the same people who once scoffed and shook their heads are now quietly sitting on the sidelines, as if they always knew Amazon would dominate e-commerce, or Tesla was bound to revolutionize the auto industry.

The critics go silent, and what was once "overvalued" becomes self-evident. Rarely do they stop to acknowledge how wrong they were... or how right you were, for seeing what they couldn't.

Funny, isn't it? The very things people once ridiculed and resisted so vehemently suddenly become... *obvious*. Time to rock Arthur Schopenhauer for a third and final time, as he sums it up perfectly here:

Truth goes through three stages. First, it is ridiculed. Second, it is violently opposed. Third, it is accepted as self-evident.

The way to maximize your returns is to buy and hold your Rule Breakers through all *three* of these stages!

Here's another way of saying it, to close for now:

If you can find...

The top dog and first-mover in an important, emerging industry.

With a sustainable competitive advantage.

Stellar past price appreciation.

Good management and smart backing.

And strong consumer appeal.

... *and,* some guy from CNBC or *The Wall Street Journal* is telling you it's:

⋯→ "OVERVALUED." ←⋯

To me? You've heard and seen all you need.

Hello, world.[73]

---

73 One of my favorite TV appearances was on PBS's *Wealthtrack* with the superb Consuelo Mack. On April 27, 2016, she pinned me down to pick one stock. I chose a Rule Breaker specifically noting how "overvalued" it was. It's aged well: tinyurl.com/2j2b397m

THE 6 TRAITS OF THE RULE BREAKER STOCK

TRAIT #1:
TOP DOG AND FIRST-MOVER IN AN IMPORTANT, EMERGING INDUSTRY.

TRAIT #2:
SUSTAINABLE COMPETITIVE ADVANTAGE.

TRAIT #3:
STELLAR PAST PRICE APPRECIATION.

TRAIT #4:
GOOD MANAGEMENT AND SMART BACKING.

TRAIT #5:
STRONG CONSUMER APPEAL.

TRAIT #6:
"OVERVALUED."

1 OO-BAGGERS ARISE FROM two sources, not one. Most obviously, there is the stock pick itself. That's what we've covered in Part II, the Six Traits I have used to find Rule Breaker market-crushers. When you see **most or all of these traits working together**, your interest should ignite.

But you won't score 100-baggers off stock picks alone! You'll only get there if you follow good habits, the Six Habits we covered in Part I.

So, *two* sources work in tandem: Rule Breaker Traits to find your stocks, and Rule Breaker Habits to hold them. Expressed mathematically, it's not Habits + Traits, but **Habits** × **Traits** that unlocks all the value the market has to offer. And the market has *a lot* to offer: The 100-baggers are out there.

And I have found them. Any one of these stocks has, on its own, empowered or fully enabled financial freedom. But beyond the picks and numbers, I take pride in demonstrating *that* this can happen. People read about others making such investments. Authors write books (this one, for instance) theorizing about winning approaches to the markets. But beyond theory is practice. It has been my pleasure and privilege not just to sit above the arena and observe, but to have been there on the field all along, back in the batter's box every month for nearly 30 years (and striking out a lot, too).

What matters most to me about this list is making it not just imaginable but real, for millions of people. Each row is special.

The prices have fluctuated since the publishing date, and these stocks will go in and out of favor. Some may fall from the 100-bagger ledge, while others near but not on the list, like Shopify, Salesforce, or Chipotle, may arrive. In the end, there is no specific magic to the number "100."

Heck, I prefer 1,371.

Company	Ticker	Pick date	Cost	12/31/2024	Gain	Bagger
Intuitive Surgical	ISRG	3/16/2005	$4.91	$521.96	10,530%	106
MercadoLibre	MELI	2/18/2009	$14.13	$1,700.44	11,934%	120
Tesla	TSLA	11/23/2011	$2.10	$403.84	19,130%	192
Booking Holdings	BKNG	5/19/2004	$23.71	$4,968.42	20,855%	209
Netflix	NFLX	12/1/2004	$1.85	$891.32	48,079%	481
Nvidia	NVDA	4/15/2005	$0.162	$134.29	82,795%	828
Amazon.com*	AMZN	9/8/1997	$0.16	$219.39	137,019%	1,371

* You might enjoy a link to the original buy report, forever free on the internet: tinyurl.com/5n94b9f3

SUMMARY OF PART II: TALE OF TWO INVESTORS

"Hi, All About Numbers. I'm Sally. I work on the Sunbeam project. What brings you here?"

That's what she'd said, and ever since that night, she and the ensuing conversation kept coming back to him, words he couldn't shake. They'd exchanged numbers but hadn't texted. Harry particularly remembered, even was haunted by, *this* exchange:

"So, how much are they aiming to raise tonight?" he'd asked. "Do you think they'll hit The Number?"

Sally had paused thoughtfully—wistfully?—then smiled, looking over at a tortoise-shaped ice sculpture. **"You know, Mr. All About Numbers, sometimes there *are* no numbers for the things that matter most."**

The following week at work, Jake poked his head in: "Did you get into the SynerTech IPO? It's supposed to hang ten today! I got one word for ya, Harry, one word," he said, pulling him aside. "*Bioplastics*!"

Harry shrugged. "Yeah, I should take a look. Though actually, Jake... I dunno. There's something... um, ever since that fundraiser last week. What was her name? Sally?"

Jake smirked. "The one with the solar panels and tortoises? She's got you rethinking your financial life after one conversation?"

Harry chuckled. "Hey, well I'll say this: I haven't looked at another IPO since."

"Another IPO, or another girl?"

"She made some good points! I regret that I called her 'Tortoise Shell' because, you know, tortoises, but really because of her Warby Parker glasses. But then she said she owns their stock. 'They've built a strong brand,' she says, 'with a social mission: buy a pair, give a pair....' I looked 'em up. Totally overvalued, of course, but they've got raving fans. Stock's up 40%, last four months!"

"Totally overvalued, huh? Yeah... like you said with Tesla... *overvalued*. All the way up," Jake quipped. "The thing I wonder about Warby though, is do they have a competitive advantage that's actually sustain—."

Just then, Harry's phone buzzed with a trading alert. The app was telling him to act now because one of his picks, pretty much his worst stock, one he'd bought a few months back, had spiked to a new low. An exciting new low, according to the app. *Plus, if he doubled down now in the next 15 minutes, he would unlock a new outfit for his online avatar.* He'd already collected almost all of those. This one was for a clown costume.

Speaking of clowns, that's how he felt these days about the stock's CEO.

Jake looked over his shoulder, seeing the stock chart. "You know, when it comes to stocks, I think you should be looking for *top* dogs, my friend, not *shaggy* dogs," Jake offered.

"Yeah, and you might be talking about the chart, right? But I'm wondering whether *that CEO* is a shaggy dog." Searching his app's list of snapshot statistics for the stock in question, Harry realized now that he couldn't find what he was really looking for. "There should be a number, in these apps, that would rate the CEOs of these companies.... And some of those numbers would be *negative*."

"Yeah?" Jake said, thinking about it. Then, completely off the cuff: "It's true. Ha! Sometimes, there are no numbers for the things that matter most...."

Meanwhile...

Sally was in her office, surrounded by reports and blueprints for the Sunbeam Solar Array project. Her friend and colleague Clara walked in with a grin. "Morning, Sally. You seem unusually chipper today. Did something happen? *Did we finally get the okay on the bifacial solar panels...?*"

Sally looked up, smiling. "Not exactly. Not that. Met someone interesting at the fundraiser last week."

"Tell!"

"He's... *different* from my usual crowd. All about short-term trading and quick gains. But there was something intriguing about him. I think I'm going to text him. But, I dunno: *Awkward*, right? What should I text?"

Clara grinned. "Just be yourself. Maybe mention something that caught your interest at the fundraiser."

Sally nodded and typed:

hey harry, tortoise shell's been thinking twice about what you said about warby p
stock's been on a roll—which to me is always a good sign—
you want in? maybe we could discuss more over spectacles
I mean, coffee

She hit send and waited, her heart beating a little faster.

Almost immediately, her phone buzzed with Harry's reply:

i'd like that
how about this weekend?

Clara peeked. "Looks like you've got yourself a coffee date!"

"Yeah, I guess I do," Sally smiled. "It's funny, Clara. Sometimes you meet someone who makes you see things differently, makes you rethink your approach."

Clara nodded. "Sounds like he's doing the same. Maybe you two will find a balance between short-term excitement, and long-term... shall we say... *vision*?" That Clara. What a wit.

Just then, a call came through on Sally's phone. She glanced at the screen and froze. "What's wrong?" Clara asked.

Sally frowned. "It's the investor from our last project. He never calls unless it's urgent." She answered the call, her voice steady.

"Hello?"

THE 6
PRINCIPLES
OF THE RULE
BREAKER
PORTFOLIO

STOCKS POP AND investors cheer. "Pops" have always meant *up*; they follow positive earnings surprises, major deals, regulatory approvals, analyst upgrades. When stocks pop (minimum +5%), who doesn't like that? (Um... short sellers.)

But there is another kind of pop. It's a word I helped invent because it needed to be. It's not yet in *Webster's*, but is in the Urban Dictionary.[74] And it got a cameo tease in Chapter O.

So sure, there are pops. But then there are *spiffy-pops*!

When a stock rises more in a single day than you paid for it, that's a spiffy-pop.

You first bought it years ago at $60. The stock has since risen to $1,000. The company announces great earnings at the morning bell, and today the stock jumps $70 to $1,070—a 7% rise. The world says it popped; we say it *spiffy-popped* because it rose more (+$70) in a single day than your cost basis ($60).

To many, that sounds unimaginable. Or at least unattainable. For Rule Breaker investors, it becomes a daily thing. It's how investing works. I didn't invent the word as a linguistic exercise; I invented it to demonstrate it, and I have demonstrated it literally thousands of times over the years.

In Part II's Finale, I said **Habits** × **Traits** equals 100-baggers. Habits × Traits also equals spiffy-pops.

And one more thing, too:

Habits × Traits gives rise to *your portfolio*. And that is our focus in Part III: **The Six Principles of the Rule Breaker Portfolio**, your guide to building and managing a portfolio that reflects your best vision for our future. These principles are the scaffolding that will support your decisions, offering both structure and freedom as you craft and grow a portfolio that truly feels like *yours*.

---

74 www.urbandictionary.com/define.php?term=spiffy%20pop; is the Urban Dictionary more in touch than Webster's?!

CHAPTER 13

MAKE YOUR PORTFOLIO REFLECT YOUR BEST VISION FOR OUR FUTURE

"So the point is not to become a leader. The point is to become yourself, to use yourself completely— all your skills, gifts, and energies—in order to make your vision manifest.... You must, in sum, become the person you started out to be, and to enjoy the process of becoming."

—WARREN BENNIS,
ON BECOMING A LEADER

WARREN BENNIS WROTE many fine books on leadership. My favorite is *On Becoming a Leader*. I recommend it to all; I quote from it regularly.

As you can see from this chapter's epigraph, his advice focuses on being who we—who you—were *meant* to be. He asserted that the number one trait of a leader was *authenticity*, becoming oneself, completely using your skills, gifts, and energies.

The same is true for your portfolio!

As you manage yourself (Part I) and pick your stocks (Part II), you should ensure that the result, *your portfolio*, does indeed "make your vision manifest." Not your broker's vision. Not that index fund that just buys everything. *Your* vision. The most important principle of the Rule Breaker Portfolio is to:

> ...→ **MAKE YOUR PORTFOLIO REFLECT YOUR BEST VISION FOR OUR FUTURE.** ←..

But I'm jumping ahead...

Let me kick off Part III by explaining how it's organized. I'm sharing with you here the Six Principles of the Rule Breaker Portfolio. Having principles to guide you in managing your portfolio is particularly valuable for the many people who never received meaningful instruction or coaching on how to run their own portfolios.

As I mentioned in the Introduction, the most frequently asked question over the years on my podcast has been, *"What's the right number of stocks for my portfolio?"* (That is the wrong question; there's no single, correct number.) I have developed these Six Principles over the years to help people ask and have answers to better questions.

Two more prefatory points:

First, notice the parallelism with my Habits and Traits. I like the number six! Half a dozen provides a robust framework, yet not so many that you lose track.[75] But **no list of Six Habits or Traits or Principles is exhaustive or airtight**. There are other habits to develop, traits to look for, and certainly more to be said about stewarding a portfolio. I can't solve everyone's portfolio construction problems with six one-liners. But Part III sets up the scaffolding you can adapt, filling in gaps with your own insights and experiences.

Second, these Six Principles are split into two groups of three: **building your portfolio** (Principles #1–#3) and **managing your portfolio**

---

75 Spoiler alert: "There is Another"—a fourth list of six, cf. The Afterword.

(Principles #4–#6). Note as well, then, that I'm not focused in this book on selling off your portfolio or shutting it down, in retirement or at the end of life. Those considerations will occasionally color what I'm saying in Part III. But my Six Principles focus on *creating and maintaining* a dynamic, growth-oriented portfolio. Yours.

Let's get started.

"YOUR"

We're going to parse language a lot for Trait #1, because every word of it counts. Let's talk about the second and fifth words: "your."

Your portfolio exists to "make your vision manifest," as Warren Bennis said. Making your portfolio truly yours gives it the best hope of winning.

Does this seem straightforward? For many, it is not.

Many people had someone else pick their strategy, probably their investments too. I want for you what we wanted for Lisa Ling. We asked her: "When you open up your fridge, Lisa, what are some of the things inside that make you smile?" You should be able to look up and down your portfolio and see companies whose purposes you believe will elevate humanity and whose names make you smile.

Which can you better commit to, learn from, and enjoy—your portfolio, or someone else's?

By reframing your thinking to make *your* portfolio reflect *your best vision for our future*, you will prosper more in every way, through the learning, the enjoyment, the fulfillment, and the performance.

"PORTFOLIO"

The third word is what Part III is all about, so let's lay out some particulars in building a portfolio:

- **Your portfolio should number 20+ stocks from the start, equally weighted** (cf. Chapter 15), dovetailing with Habit #5: 5% max initial position! This ensures you begin with a broad base, and no single stock exerts undue influence over your results or psychology.

- **You should be able to look up and down your portfolio and feel confident**: You know what the companies do, you have intentions and expectations about their future, and you believe that our collective future will be better as they succeed.
- **Your portfolio should feature companies of different sizes (small, medium, large) working in different industries**, so your portfolio is not overinvested in a single trend or sector.
- **Every stock in your portfolio is an *investment*, held for at least three years.** We've covered this. Just ensure your portfolio reflects it. Now, if you want to take a flier on just a stock or two, you *can* play inside three years. Go ahead; you have my permission. (Just don't tell anyone I said that.) Call them exceptions that prove the rule.
- **If you have dividends coming in, reinvest them unless you really need the income.** Using dividends to buy more shares compounds your wealth over time. It's like planting *money trees*: Each reinvested dividend is a seed that grows into more shares, which produce more dividends. Over time, your portfolio flourishes, a forest of money trees!

A word or two about what's missing above. You don't see me urging you to diversify geographically. I have a "go anywhere" mentality when picking stocks, and a "no forced march" policy into areas outside your interest and expertise. So yes, we go where there's greatness (often the United States, but there are worldbeaters globally). We *don't* need to invest in certain geographies or sectors because someone told us to have "more money in emerging markets" or minimum allocations to sectors ("5% allocated to hot-dog stands").

You also don't see emphasis on rebalancing, which we'll talk further about in Chapter 16.

Back in the day, we used to give additional prescriptive advice (for instance, how to open a brokerage account); things were more complicated then. Today, whether you're using a smartphone app like Robinhood or visiting your local Schwab office, opening an account is easier and cheaper than ever. We've reached an era of low-to-no commissions when buying and selling stocks. And also an era where you can buy *parts* of shares (fractional shares) rather than having to pony up the money to buy full shares. (With 34 S&P 500 stocks costing $500+ a share as of this writing, being able to buy part shares makes the market accessible to all.) Starting your portfolio is simple. And oh so rewarding.

"YOUR BEST VISION"

When I first shared Principle #1 on my podcast in January 2021, I got a nice note from a friend and prominent investor, a public figure some readers would recognize (I'm omitting his name).

He said that hearing, once again, "Make your portfolio reflect your best vision for our future" changed how he thinks about investing, influencing his fund management and public advice. He didn't elaborate, but I'm guessing what struck him was the idea that **everything is connected**. The money you commit as a Rule Breaker investor goes into companies you esteem. Over time, as those companies prosper, so will the world, in a way of your choosing. Sadly, not all will (you'll have many losers!), but the best ones will, and mightily so. Your capital shapes the future in ways even invisible to us.

This is true as consumers too. By giving money to one vendor or brand over another, you shape the future in small ways daily. But this is even truer of your investment dollars, which over your life will far outnumber what you spend. Your vision, *your best vision*, will manifest in the world through your investments. Everything is connected.

And we all see different things, have different hopes. One person's consumer or investment choice differs from someone else's, sometimes starkly (like choosing between expensive renewable energy and cheaper fossil fuels). I will know some readers of this book, but most I will never meet. So I likely don't know *your* best vision of the future! That's why I'm not being prescriptive about what should be in your portfolio. What I'm telling you is that **your portfolio should reflect your best vision for our future**.

If you were to show your portfolio statement to a spouse, your grandkids, your broker, or your investment club, *they should see you in it*.

Just as our bookshelves convey our passions and interests to visitors,[76] so should your portfolio. That's Rule Breaker Investing at its core.

There are even great stocks for anti-capitalists! In 2015, I became interested in a media company struggling to shift from its old-world business model. My best vision was that this company, with its respected brand and fact-checking rigors, could rise above the "fake news" era and evolve into a successful digital subscription model (despite my own misgivings about its bias against capitalism, even conscious capitalism). So, that December, I picked the stock for Motley Fool Stock Advisor at $12.35. As of this writing, New York Times Company (NYT) has crested $52, up over 300% (the S&P 500 rose 200% over the same period). The company made the shift, and the stock has quadrupled. Now, I expect some who are reading this wouldn't want New York Times in their portfolio. In which case let me say, hey, if you don't like *The New York Times* (or Fox News, what have you), don't buy the stock!

...→ MAKE YOUR PORTFOLIO REFLECT ←... YOUR BEST VISION FOR OUR FUTURE.

"FUTURE"

The iconic 1982 movie *Blade Runner*, starring Harrison Ford and Rutger Hauer, presented a dim view of a dystopian future. History shows that sci-fi writers almost always lean dark and dystopian with their visions. There's logic behind this; if it were all peaches and cream, where's the drama?

One can argue that Hollywood's negative depictions of the future help us guard against bad outcomes. From this point of view, future-fear-mongering is future-proofing. While I can appreciate this to a point, I confess to some exhaustion at the predictably negative vibes surrounding our tales of the future. Maybe they really do expect a *Blade Runner*

---

76 Our books are our friends.

ambiance, reflected in many other shows like *The Handmaid's Tale*, *Westworld*, and *Black Mirror*. Maybe we're all headed toward those neon-lit, rain-soaked streets bustling with ominous flying cars and shadowy figures, waiting in the dark, just out of sight.

Turns out, though, not even Los Angeles was. As you probably know, and as I enjoy reminding my pessimistic friends, *Blade Runner* was set in Los Angeles in 2019. Fast forward to the actual 2019, and the denizens of Sunset Boulevard were more concerned with avocado toast and selfie sticks than replicants and flying cars. (Turns out, dystopia was postponed for brunch.) One of my favorite lessons from Matt Ridley's book *The Rational Optimist* is that humans have harbored apocalyptic, gloom-and-doom thoughts with every passing generation for centuries, and they just keep not coming true.[77]

By most measures that count for humanity, the world has been getting better over the decades: massive reductions in world poverty, infant mortality, illiteracy, infectious diseases, and malnutrition, alongside rises in life expectancy, education, and access to technology. Want more proof? Look at the stock market's long-term movements: lower-left to upper-right, despite countless calamitous predictions (and real calamities, too).

Blade Runner has always been on the horizon. Even as 2019 approached, what was hitting theaters? *Blade Runner 2049* (released in 2017). The can keeps getting kicked, another half-century ahead.[78]

This matters because the last word of Principle #1 is "future." The future is all that matters for your portfolio. Everything else has already happened; what happens *next* for your stocks determines your performance.

Two conditions are critical to maximize Rule Breaker Investing. First, take your seat in the sailboat (remember?)—not the canoe, not the rowboat—having ensured the stocks in your portfolio are positioned to prosper over the *next* 10+ years. Good portfolios are driven by looking through the windshield, not the rear-view mirror. Second, **embrace**

---

77   A generation earlier, the same lesson was taught when 1984 finally happened... not exactly like Orwell's.

78   As I write, Amazon Studios is already setting up for *Blade Runner 2099*....

optimism, harbor *positive* thoughts about our future.[79] Positivity about the future will run contrary to much of our culture's doom-scrolling worries—and that's why it works. Breaking the rules is lucrative in part *because* you're defying convention. As your oddly optimistic views are proven right, you'll have made multiple times your money.

So yes, making your portfolio reflect a positive vision of the future will very likely be both more accurate and profitable than following others' "game over, man" thoughts. Winning this way, you'll echo the experiences of optimistic investors and entrepreneurs who've similarly won over the past few hundred years.[80] I'm in the *Gone With the Wind* camp when we think about tomorrow; with Scarlett O'Hara, I believe "tomorrow is another day." But I feel even more positively about it than Scarlett. I believe **tomorrow will be a better day**, and today's stock market valuations often fail to account for this. We Rule Breakers keep buying mispriced securities—mispriced because they're dramatically UNDERPRICED, else we wouldn't be packing 10-baggers, 50-baggers, 100+-baggers over just a decade or two.

Speaking of packing, the Rule Breaker winning approach packs a fantastic one–two combination. First, other people find our stocks "Overvalued" (Trait #6, Chapter 12). That's the left jab. But then, second, the right uppercut is powered by a mass perception that society's going in the wrong direction, threats are everywhere, the economy's going to melt down, and the market will crash. (Again.) There is some truth to these things, and you've likely lived through it. The problem is it's all fear-based, it compounds on itself, and it's made to sound final. Forget about your portfolio: *We're all doomed!*[81]

Starting in 2013 I have driven my Tesla around my native city of

---

79 Think about all of us, not just your own future. Be expansive, it'll help. That's why I say *"our* future."

80 … years which have included many horrendous things all the way through, like wars and genocide and financial crashes and lots of crime, too. I'm not here to sugar-coat anything. The more we can reduce these things in future, the (even) better our market returns will be.

81 "There is seduction in apocalyptic thinking. If one lives in the Last Days, one's actions, one's very life, take on historical meaning and no small measure of poignance." —Eric Zencey

Washington, DC. The license plate of my car (honk if you see me) is where I try to keep my portfolio positioned, my mind too: FUTURE.

William Gibson once wrote, "The future's already here; it's just not evenly distributed." Driving a Tesla around the nation's capital surrounded by older cars, gas stations, aging infrastructure, and sometimes smoggy air, I felt like I was back from the future—a sign you're in a good place as an investor. Driving in FUTURE, I also held Tesla stock—all the way up from 2011. That it rose more than 100 times was extremely confirming, especially given how "overvalued" and highly shorted it was... in such a broken and troubled world.

MULTIPLE FUTURES

One more thing about "Future." The strongest, most principled Rule Breaker Portfolios embrace stocks with many different potential futures. The Chief Investment Officer at The Motley Fool, my friend Andy Cross, once opened my eyes as to how Rule Breaker Investing contrasts with Warren Buffett's investing style. It was the late 1990s, and Andy articulated it in a way that's helped me explain what I do ever since: "In his companies, Buffett is looking for one sure future," Andy said, "whereas, David, you love companies with multiple futures."

The future is a fork in the road. Every company at this fork contemplates multiple path options that will ultimately translate to their one actual future. Andy was saying that Buffett loves companies that basically just have one path, one option, "forever businesses" like insurance (GEICO) and chocolate (See's Candies). Businesses like GEICO and See's tread simple paths. "When you get to the fork in the road, take it," is one of the better-known Yogi Berra witticisms, and yet it is perfectly accurate for these kinds of companies! They don't pivot, don't have much need or ambition to do so. Many investors love the energizer bunnies of business that just keep going, and going, and going....

But in Chapter 10, I shared with you this maxim: **"Go with the business that is opening up yet more options for itself."** This is the opposite side of the coin, favoring the Rule Breakers, their optionality, favoring innovation and the chaos (unpredictability) of it, being okay with the "not knowing."

A classic, memorable case-in-point contrast is this Bloomberg article from 2011, headlined: "Buffett to Extend Aversion Toward Apple, Electronics Makers." It begins:

> Warren Buffett said he'll probably prolong his aversion to electronics makers such as Apple Inc. because their business prospects are harder to predict than companies such as Coca-Cola Co.
>
> 'We held very few in the past and we're likely to hold very few in the future,' the billionaire chairman of Berkshire Hathaway Inc. said in Daegu, South Korea, today, referring to electronics makers. Coca-Cola, based in Atlanta, is 'very easy for me to come to a conclusion as to what it will look like economically in five or 10 years, and it's not easy for me to come to a conclusion about Apple,' he said.

I first picked Apple as a true-blue Rule Breaker for Motley Fool Stock Advisor on January 18, 2008. (Still holding.) I felt like I might be a little late! The company had launched the iPhone the year before. But I was personally making the shift from Windows to Mac,[82] and Apple checked all six of my Rule Breaker Trait boxes. "Let's go!" I thought.

And it has. As of this writing, the stock pick is up 51 times.

By contrast, Buffett's 2011 statement about staying in Coca-Cola and avoiding Apple was consistent with his logic and history. And the Warren Buffett Way has worked wonderfully! *Yet there are other ways*, based on different logic and choices that sometimes even go opposite the "Oracle of Omaha."

---

82   Reason #1: I hated "Windows phone" options. Reason #2: My teenaged daughter Kate, always an innovator in our family, had just bought a MacBook—a family first. Having been a PC guy for 30 years before that, I needed to figure out Apple as I was her first line of tech support! Parents can relate.

Since the article cited above, Apple is up 21 times in value. Coca-Cola has doubled.[83]

The average mid-cap company has three to five futures; large caps, only two or three. You might expect the opposite, that the bigger you get, the more choices you have? Not really. Talk to an aircraft carrier captain.

But Rule Breaker companies are different. On average, I would say they have eight to 20 futures—eight to 20 paths at the fork, each featuring different risks and rewards, half of which aren't even foreseeable or easily predictable! Probably the greatest example of all today is Alphabet, whose holding-company structure lets it simultaneously pioneer fields from AI and autonomous driving to next-generation healthcare, all funded by Google's enormous profits. But across every industry, when you focus on "who is the innovator," you'll find most of the great companies of our time, collectively possessing infinite futures, which (yes, Andy Cross) I prefer to just one.

Enough with the *future*—my favorite word. Back to portfolios.

HENRIK'S T-SHIRT TEST

A wonderful mental picture to guide you as you make your portfolio reflect your best vision for our future comes from my friend Henrik and his T-shirt test. Henrik, a Rule Breaker from Germany, wrote me this in 2022:

> Hey David, I've been thinking about your definition of being an investor, derived from Latin meaning 'to clothe,' and I think my test—'would I proudly wear the logo of the company I'm about to invest in, big and bold on a t-shirt for everyone to see'—is a nice addition to your Snap Test.
>
> If a company leaves the world better, promotes important values like equality and dignity, champions conscious capitalism, and can crush the market long-term, I'd proudly wear its logo and invest

---

83   The big joke here is that while many Fools like me still own Apple, and it's up dozens of times in value, Buffett eventually accumulated a stake in Apple worth more than $100 billion. *He changed his mind.* (Many of us do have a way lower cost basis, though!)

in it. Conversely, if a company fails these criteria (e.g., promoting toxic masculinity or mistreating stakeholders), I wouldn't wear its logo or invest in it.

I'd love to hear your thoughts on my test (I need a better name for it). All the best, and Fool on!—Henrik

Henrik gets it! He combined my etymology breakdown of *investire* (cf. Chapter 3, *putting on the jersey*) with the Snap Test (cf. Chapter 4, *would anyone notice... would anyone care?*) to home-brew a master-class solution. It's a challenge we can all embrace, maybe each day for a month: **Would you proudly wear the T-shirt of every company you're invested in?**

Ideally, that challenge shouldn't be very challenging. It should be fun. "Making your vision manifest" will keep you grounded and feel satisfying, especially when you win. Whether as a fun monthly challenge or just a helpful mental picture, Henrik's T-Shirt Test (*that's the name, Henrik!*) helps you keep our most important portfolio principle, Principle #1, firmly in mind:

→ **MAKE YOUR PORTFOLIO REFLECT YOUR BEST VISION FOR OUR FUTURE.** ←

CHAPTER 14

KNOW AND NAME ITS PURPOSE

W HY ARE YOU doing this? Why are you building a portfolio? The default assumption that you're investing money in a nest egg to grow it as big as possible will ring true for many, me included. But it's not always true. Some people want to:

- start a portfolio for a grandchild to teach them to love investing
- earn steady, reliable income
- benefit planet Earth by investing in companies that treat her well
- have fun (?) speculating on cryptocurrencies
- create a never-ending philanthropic legacy

In the case of the first, teaching a grandchild a lifelong love of investing should prioritize picking stocks they understand and enjoy. Teaching kids they can become part owners of brands they love—an eye-opener for me in my youth—takes precedence over maximizing financial appreciation. Similarly, building a portfolio for reliable income necessitates trading off some outperformance for steady cash flow. Thus, being clear from the get-go about *why* this portfolio exists, and what master it will serve, constitutes Principle #2:

··→ KNOW AND NAME ITS PURPOSE. ←··

My default portfolio purpose has been to maximize overall appreciation.[84] And when your portfolio truly reflects your best vision for our future, I believe you're *better* positioned for maximum performance. But given a multiplicity of possible purposes, and how these in turn relate to *goals*, it's worth going deeper and drawing some distinctions.

I believe most people think more in terms of goals than purpose. Goals can be quick to dream up, providing a measurable amount ("the minimum I'll need to retire") or date ("I want to be financially free by age XX"). That said, goals don't always fit: Can you set a goal that enables you to quantify, to know for sure, whether your grandchild *has* developed a habit and love of investing? Maybe! Maybe not. An income portfolio might have a goal to find stocks with a 3% or higher dividend yield that have low volatility, but whether those stocks do in fact exhibit a low market beta is a roll of the dice. So goals can be set, but not met; the act of making a goal is an act of faith, of hope.

Setting purpose, on the other hand, is an act of will and intention. That's why I favor purpose and purpose-driven constructs (here, a portfolio). When I set a purpose I am in control of that, and my purpose guides me to fulfillment.

Setting a purpose and setting goals are not mutually exclusive. Goals can be incredibly effective when they're set out as scorekeepers, or signposts along the path. A lot of financial planning and publishing is designed around setting goals, especially portfolio goals, with numbers and dates. That's why I think it's a bit Rule Breaker-y, instead, to set a purpose. As someone who has pretty much never set financial goals for my investing, I have nevertheless outperformed all my dreams—in part because I pursued purpose, and let my dreams guide me.

So for any portfolio you set up for yourself or for others, think hard about its purpose. What, and whom, does it stand for? Getting clear on that up front makes it easier to invest the rest of the way, whatever your

---

84   I articulated this in my 2005 Motley Fool article, "The Highest Possible Returns. Period." tinyurl.com/2w2r6mdv

goals, and whatever the world throws at you (black swans for good, or ill, included).

ODYSSEY OR PHOENIX?

Probably the biggest driver of portfolio purpose hinges on *whether there will be new money coming in or not*. In my parlance, I ask, "Is it an *Odyssey* or a *Phoenix*?"[85]

Odyssey portfolios typify those of younger people, the wage-earners, strivers, adventurers with a lot ahead of them, with new money coming in all the time. As I've shared throughout, if this is you, you should always be saving and investing, *riding the rollercoaster*, dollar-cost-averaging as you go. Let the money accumulate over a couple weeks or months, whatever rhythm works best, and invest. Rinse and repeat. You're likely purposing financial freedom (some call it "retirement"). You're not there yet, so you're on an Odyssey.

Or are you a *Phoenix*? The phoenix is the mythical bird that, at the end of its life, lights up in flames and is reborn from its ashes. For me, that's a catchy metaphor for those older in life, perhaps newly retired. They're beautifully reborn, usually alongside their approach to money, as "retired" generally means no new money coming in. My Motley Fool colleague Jim Mueller oversaw a Phoenix portfolio service for members, given a single lump sum to invest, and draw income from, using Rule Breaker stocks.

Jim emphasized being *slow to sell*—really slow, like glacial. Problems periodically arise in long-term holdings. Short sellers swoop in, journalists too, and the stock drops. This can look scary. But if management's any good—and if you're adhering to Trait #4, it should be!—they likely see it and are already addressing it.[86]

Jim cited Panera Bread as a selling mistake he made. In 2014, Panera faced operational inefficiencies and lower marks for customer experience.

---

85 These were the very terms we used to name our portfolios back when I helped oversee The Motley Fool's old Supernova services. Gentlemen, it has been said, prefer blondes. Literature majors prefer myths.

86 Think about AOL's young CEO Steve Case in Chapter 10.

It announced "Panera 2.0" to launch digital ordering, improve food preparation, and enhance customer service. He sold half the position early in these changes, as they weren't yet reflected in the numbers, and the price and sentiment were down. Not much more than a year later, Panera was taken private by JAB Holding Company at about double the price!

Another insight from Jim: If you have a big winner in your lump-sum Phoenix portfolio, don't hesitate to milk it for cash, either to reallocate to other holdings or to live off the proceeds. This goes against Habit #1, of course, but in a lump-sum portfolio whose purpose is to enable you to live out your days without financial worry, your greatest sources of capital to live on are your big winners. Don't be afraid to pare them down over time. Having a cash cushion of around 10% can ease the stress when you need to start selling. If the market retreats, it feels better to live off of some of that cash than to sell some of your best stocks at temporarily "on sale" prices. While this book isn't meant to provide retirement portfolio advice, the key takeaway is that **articulating and adhering to your portfolio's purpose are valuable acts**, giving you a clear lens as you gaze at your investments, and at the world.

There's a natural tendency to think that Rule Breaker Investing suits Odysseys better than Phoenixes, and I generally agree. History, however, shows that Motley Fool *Odyssey* and *Phoenix* portfolios—one constantly buying, the other selling quarterly—both substantially whomped the market averages.

A final thought on purposefully building a portfolio. Just as every investor has a lifecycle, so does every business. These cycles often align with one another. Generally, older people do well to invest in longer-standing, established companies that they've known over their lives. Conversely, younger people do well to consider newer, upstart companies, the Rule Breakers that are looking to disrupt the Rule Makers.

These are mass generalizations, admitting many exceptions. Recalling again the Pirate's Code from *Pirates of the Caribbean*, they're really just guidelines.

NAMES

And that phrase, *really just guidelines*, sums up well the whole of Part III.

Part I is intentionally *prescriptive*; I am convinced that mass adoption of the Six Habits will lead to better returns. Part II is *assertive*; I am reasserting the traits that have consistently enabled me to score 100-baggers through diverse market conditions since the mid-1990s. But if Part I is prescriptive and Part II is assertive, Part III is *suggestive*. There are too many factors to consider in building and maintaining a portfolio. That's why naming Six Principles, a principles-based approach, seems best.

I've thus far only spoken to half this chapter's title, about Knowing Its Purpose. Let me close with the "Name" part. Names (Odyssey and Phoenix, for example) ground us in our purpose and help us adhere to it. Without stating our purpose at the outset, and naming it, we can lose focus and get carried away. After a great market year, we might start speculating out of proportion with our original intentions. After a horrible market downdraft, we might stop investing altogether, concluding that stocks picked with a clear eye and conscience were a huge mistake—you're doomed.

Ah, but if you had named your portfolio "Grandpa's Generational Gems," you're much less likely to take stupid or greedy risks! Or if you'd named your portfolio "Sally's Sunshine Stocks," you're much less likely to give up! This is especially true, in both cases, if you've shared and socialized these names with friends and family.

Names serve as north stars to bring us back to our original rational thinking, not overreacting to subsequent conditions.

What's in a name? Shakespeare's Juliet says, "That which we call a rose by any other name would smell as sweet." But I think names are more powerful than that. In fact, had she named her plan to fake her death "Project Rebirth" and shared it with trusted allies beyond just the Friar, that name alone might have changed Juliet's fate![87]

---

[87] Mayhap *Romeo and Juliet*'s greatest tragedy is that Shakespeare omitted any Fool character from this one, who could have proffered this advice!

So yeah, I'm here to suggest all kinds of wrongs can be righted—if, in building your portfolio, you:

··→ **KNOW AND NAME ITS PURPOSE.** ←··

CHAPTER 15

FAIR STARTING LINE

I HAVE ALWAYS HAD a love of the horse track, a reflection of my mother's tastes. I can't ride horses like she could, given my lifelong allergy to them. And I certainly don't think you should spend much money betting on them. But the jockeys' colors, the flair of the derby, the festive crowds, the horses' racing numbers (lower numbers being advantageous, by the way, as they put horses closer to the inside of the track), and their odds.... *The separate but connected factors of horse and rider*. All of these hold a romantic allure for me, an ineffable fun that rings out like the clarion call of the "First Call" bugle.

The Motley Fool started in 1993 as a home-brew paper newsletter sold to friends and family (they were the only ones who'd foot us the $48 annual subscription for an enterprise of questionable merit). It lasted one year in print before the internet started, so we've since taken to calling it Ye Olde Printed Foole.

Ye Olde Printed Foole adopted horse racing as its graphical theme: Each stock we picked was a horse, and our pages featured cartoons and doodles depicting thoroughbreds (our winners) and mules. When we sold a stock it went off to pasture, or if it had been a bad one (and there were many in our early days), we'd joke darkly about glue factories.

Investing and racing share many parallels (cf. Principle #5, two chapters hence), whether we're talking about fields of winners and losers, putting odds on success, relating numbers and colors to ticker symbols, analyzing past performance, considering track (or market) conditions, and predicting outcomes. Also, of course, the sheer excitement of putting down your money and seeing what happens! Though admittedly, horse races are far more immediately thrilling. And a lot less consequential.

So it's easy to step into the spirit of Churchill Downs for this chapter, and I encourage you to do so as well. Don that bright bonnet, drag out a colorful old tie (remember when gentlemen used to wear ties?), take a sip of a mint julep (blech—what do people see in these?). Because every investor building a portfolio can learn a valuable lesson taught and re-taught every time you spend a day at the races:

···→ FAIR STARTING LINE. ←···

THE WINNER'S CIRCLE...

Picture the start of the Kentucky Derby.

Equidistant from the finish line, there are typically 20 horses in 20 different gates.[88] Every horse has a fair starting line—Principle #3, the third and last of my portfolio building principles (#4–#6 are about maintenance and management).

Launching this new portfolio you're building is akin to those exciting few moments before the starting bell. You're lining up your stocks, calming them (and yourself), putting them in their places, neck and neck. You likely have more confidence in some than others; looking across your line of 20-ish, you know your favorites and your long-shots. But every horse has a shot. And anyone who's watched horses circle tracks—or, our planet circle the sun enough times—knows that some of your favorites will go lame, and some dark horses will surprise you. In the Kentucky Derby of your own portfolio, you want presumed Secretariats (odds 3–2

---

88   The past ten years have featured 20 more often than any other number, with the lowest being a Covid-reduced 15. I love that 20 is the mode, because that perfectly fits with Habit #5, 5% Max Initial Position. Rules of thumb that feature round numbers, and consistency across contexts, are the best.

in 1973—he won) and a Rich Strike or two in there as well (odds 80–1 in 2022—he won). You've assembled all these stocks, given each a fair starting line, and you're seconds from the race's (the New York Stock Exchange's) starting bell.

However... *pause* for a moment.

With Principle #1, I emphasized making your portfolio reflect your best vision for our future. But for many of us, that vision can be unbalanced—tilted toward a specific outcome, technology, or industry. Our imaginations and knowledge are naturally more focused in certain areas, not evenly spaced across 20 independent thoughts or 20 different sectors. So before the starting bell, there's often a temptation to load up on your favorites.

Don't do it!

Almost every time I've over-allocated to an initial position, I've been wrong. At the beating heart of the instinct to load up is usually greed, which we must guard against most. My worst investments have been when I backed up the truck—specifically employing the little bit of private (venture capital) investment I've allocated, thinking, "I want to own a *lot* of this promising start-up!" I've done my research, and at the outset, things look so promising....

For any angel or early-stage venture investment I've ever made, I should have divided the amount into five *and spread that to four other startups*.

Dan Pink, in his book *The Power of Regret*, encourages us to acknowledge our regrets. Instead of saying, "I got no regrets" (which can't be true), we should reflect on our past and identify, name, and share our regrets.

I'm sharing one of mine: sometimes over-allocating (to early-stage ventures). Part of why Rich Strike was such a rich strike is that very few long-shots ever make it. So: Don't do it!

Okay, fast-forwarding for now to the end of the race (minimum three years, preferably three decades), **you're much more likely to be surprised, than not, by *who's* in the Winner's Circle.** So's everybody else, too. If everyone knew who'd be there, no surprises or big payoffs would ensue. Chances are, you won't have a clear idea until years later about which of your Rule Breaker stocks will have crushed it, and which got crushed. (Both will happen.)

That's why most people in the Winner's Circle of life don't risk huge amounts on a single outcome. They spread their bets. (At the outset, at least....)

... IS YOUR CIRCLE OF COMPETENCE: GROW IT

Speaking of circles, Warren Buffett has famously championed a related idea: one's circle of competence. An imaginary perimeter drawn around yourself, your circle of competence contains inside it all the things that you know, love, and care about... areas where you're competent. **Your money should be inside that circle, too.**

Risking meaningful amounts of money outside your circle of competence, which too many people do? Big mistake. *Why forsake home-field advantage?!* You're forgetting the color of your home jersey.

The circle of competence is a guiding light for all of us as we think about how to invest our precious savings (and our precious time).

Just above, I mentioned that greed is often at the core of overloading on positions. But for some people that's not the case. There's another reason investors mistakenly overload positions: They simply don't have enough other good investment ideas. So they buy a few stocks, putting big hopes and big money into one or two of them. Some do it by intention as experienced "focused investors," but most do it because they're new or inexperienced. Coming up with 20 stock ideas is too much.

As much as I love investing in individual stocks, and believe that *everyone should own at least one stock*, I've said since we launched The Fool that you should allocate to index funds as needed to ensure you're not over-allocating to any one stock, and can sleep at night. I'll speak more on this next chapter with Principle #4, but **index funds are our friends and can take up as big a slice of your portfolio pie as needed**. Fair starting line pertains to your stock investments; broadly diversified funds can fill the rest, providing stability and reducing risk.

But there's another way to compensate for too few stock ideas, if your best vision for our future isn't big enough:

Your circle of competence isn't fixed!

Remember Archbishop William Temple's line from Chapter 10:

"The greater the island of knowledge, the longer the coastline of mystery."[89] The more we learn, the more we realize how much we don't know. Curiosity pulls us forward—it's the story of the human race. I hope intellectual curiosity not only burns your whole life long but also fuels your portfolio. I challenge you to expand your circle of competence.

So yes, the Winner's Circle looks like an ever-widening circle of competence. Include bleeding-edge topics like genomics, artificial intelligence, renewable energy, cybersecurity, and quantum computing. No one is an expert on all these things. I'm a lifelong generalist and a Fool. I know people who know more than I do about almost everything I can think of. But that's never dissuaded me from investing (while often, ironically, the experts themselves don't!). You don't have to be an expert; you just need to be interested. Conversant. Interested and conversant will lead to competence. Keep extending your perimeter.

An ever-expanding island of knowledge is invaluable to your investing. It ensures you avoid the common mistake of buying too few investments and overloading them, not only out of greed, but because you didn't have enough ideas to spread your money around.

THE GARDNER-KRETZMANN CONTINUUM

Way back in the book's Introduction, I mentioned the most common question from new listeners of my Rule Breaker Investing podcast: "What's the right number of stocks for my portfolio?" I said then: "No such number. We'll talk about this later." Well, later has arrived.

If you're following Habit #5, max 5% initial allocation, you're already aiming for at least 20 stocks. And adhering to Principle #3, you also now know to keep your opening positions (relatively) balanced.

In which case, whether you have 20 stocks, or 70, or 150, *there is no right or wrong number.* Because all three of those numbers put big fat

---

89 Turns out it may have been first iterated by American radio personality Ralph Sockman: "The larger the island of knowledge, the longer the coastline of wonder." Nice. But I prefer the English version.

checkmarks in the boxes for max 5% initial position with a fair starting line. That's why I said: "No such number." Choose your own adventure.

Ah, but for those still looking for more guidance, let me share what spontaneously came to life the week of March 28, 2018. At the podcast microphone, I was joined by longtime Foolish friend and employee David Kretzmann. We were answering a listener's mailbag question when David surprised me by revealing that he had about 70 stocks in his portfolio.

In one sense, I shouldn't have been shocked. Haven't I just dedicated this chapter to saying that as long as you're giving a fair starting line to 20+ stocks in your portfolio, the actual number of stocks doesn't matter?

"You just shocked me with the number of stocks you own," I said to him on air. "I love it. What was that number again?"

"It's close to 70. I haven't done an exact count, but it's a lot."

"Here's a new thing: We're going to debut a term on this podcast. I don't know if it will stand the test of time. (Will it even survive this one podcast?) Let's call it **the Gardner-Kretzmann Continuum**."

"I like it."

"And the Continuum posits that **you should have roughly the same number of stocks as the number of years you've lived on this Earth**... I'm a fairly good example of this. I'm 51 and, indeed, I have approximately 51 stocks in my portfolio. David, you have blatantly violated it. You are an... idiosyncratic creature."

"I'm just playing ahead... that's all it comes down to."

"How old are you?"

"I'm 25."

"... and you have *70* stocks! You are breaking the Gardner-Kretzmann Continuum!" (There was a disturbance in the Force.)

"I'm ready for retirement, David. What can I say?"

"That is tremendous."

And it is. What a strong, foundational base for an investor that young, rocking that kind of diversity. You think he's sweating one of his companies blowing an earnings report?

Through subsequent improv, David and I refined our creation. First, we shortened it to the "GKC." I was happy to do this, having intentionally chosen a needlessly convoluted, Wall Street-style term for comic effect—a wink at how complexity often masks *utter simplicity.*

We also took it one step further, turning it into a ratio, with the number of stocks you own as the numerator and your age as the denominator, suggesting that a ratio of 1.0 or higher is the goal (51+ stocks if you're 51). Anything higher is fine, even laudable maybe, but anything lower suggests you're not giving your portfolio the diversity (and cushion against volatility) it deserves.

So, to have 70 stocks at age 25 was off-the-charts crazy (in a great way). David's GKC was 2.8!

(We showed you ours. What's yours?)

Rule Breaker readers and fans now have a simple new benchmark to aim at, for those previously wondering, "What's the right number of stocks for my portfolio?"

GKC, baby. One point oh.

BUYING IN THIRDS

Now that you've been initiated into the Gardner-Kretzmann Continuum, I'll go you one further. Let's talk about buying in thirds.

So, you've found a stock to add to your portfolio, and you've earmarked $3,000 for it. That's your go-to, fair-starting-line number.

But....

It's a Rule Breaker. It's volatile! It's at all-time highs, and everyone says it's overvalued (they've probably been saying that all the way up). Plunging $3,000 of your hard-earned savings into this stock right now feels too risky.

Do it!

Do it. But if it feels too hard, do it in the way I figured out with my first great stock, America Online. AOL looked like a world-beater early on, its stock surging, everyone calling it overvalued. As a young Fool, I wasn't fully confident this was a good idea. It had already doubled over the one year I'd been watching it! I am eternally grateful that my younger self figured out a mental hedge that enabled me to score my first monster winner.

I took my money, divided it in three, and invested like this:

First third: Buy now. Right away. No questions asked.

Second third: One month or quarter after, buy. Whatever the price.

Third third: One month or quarter after that, buy. Whatever the price.

I call this **buying in thirds**. It is an incredibly effective win-win way to get invested in any volatile stock that's trading high.

Let's do a slow-motion instant replay to see why and how this works:

Go back to that $3,000. First, split it in three: $1,000 each.

Next, invest $1,000 today. Avert your gaze, if needed, as you tap "BUY" on your smartphone or computer mouse. Just do it. (It only hurts a little while.) You are now invested!

With your remaining two-thirds, repeat the process on the same day of the next month, quarter, or whatever time increment works for you. We'll call it "the 14th of the month." *Whatever the stock has done*, one month later, do the exact same thing. If you put in $1,000 on July 14th, put in $1,000 more on August 14th, and *whatever the stock has done*, the final $1,000 goes in on September 14th.

By buying in thirds, you get fully invested at your fair-starting-line number, accomplishing over three months what you may never have done on any given day. This is exactly what I did with AOL. Watching my investment rise 150 times in value over the next six years taught me an invaluable life lesson, even though I was initially hesitant to fully commit.[90]

Some call it the progress principle, emphasizing the power of making incremental progress toward a goal. Others refer to it as the foot-in-the-door technique, where small initial commitments lead to larger ones over time. Essentially, it's dollar-cost-averaging. But I call it buying in thirds.

I don't use this method every time. Studies show that you actually make less money over time if you systematically buy in thirds. Why? Well, as the market tends to rise over time, building in delays means paying an opportunity cost: You could have been fully invested from the beginning.

---

90   I don't count AOL as one of my 100-baggers, today. I mean it was, it absolutely was (for a while)! A phenomenal investment that taught me so much, whose shares I later sold off at points (to fund my own company), or gave away. To me, a 100-bagger is an investment that crosses that line and never goes back. Following the Time Warner merger in 2000, AOL was never the same.

However, as I've built and managed my portfolios, especially with Rule Breaker stocks, I've often been happy to sacrifice a little short-term gain to get fully invested over time.[91] Here's the win-win psychology that has always comforted me during the process of buying in thirds. You win either way:

If the stock keeps rising like a rocket, you think, "Okay, it just kept going up. I'm so glad I started getting invested when I did!"

If the stock drops or nosedives, you think, "Okay, it *was* overheated and due for a breather. I'm glad I didn't put all my money in at once!" (With each succeeding third for a dropping stock, you're getting a better and better price.)

In either scenario, you're fully invested, which is the goal. You're building your portfolio. For some stocks, it'll be easy right away, while for others, you might want to stagger your buys over time (you could buy in halves or fifths as you like—no magic to thirds). But in every case, you're giving each position a:

⋯→ FAIR STARTING LINE. ←⋯

I have now covered the first three Principles of the Rule Breaker Portfolio. First, you make your portfolio reflect your best vision for our future. You recognize its purpose, determine whether you'll be adding new money regularly (a flexible portfolio) or working with a set amount (a fixed portfolio), and name it. You put in the research, mount a thoroughgoing hunt for the Six Traits to find your 20+ thoroughbreds, which are now trotting out to their gates as we speak (20+ stocks, or fewer if you supplement with funds). You're giving them a fair starting line: You neither fully trust a few of your bucking stallions champing at the bit, nor feel

---

91 Do you remember all those Rule Breaker stock charts from Chapter 9 showing huge rises *before* we finally plinked down our money?

willing to put your full money down on that purple-capped jockey riding #8. No problem: You can ease into these investments by buying in thirds.

The portfolio is assembled. The track is ready, blue skies abound. Cue the "Call to Post," maestro…!

And, as the bugle's last note fades into echo, you know what comes next. The starting bell for the rest of your investing life.

A dead clean silence of indeterminate length ensues. It won't be long.

[*BELL*]

And we're off.

CHAPTER 16

ESTABLISH YOUR SLEEP NUMBER

A S SOON AS you launch a portfolio of 20+ investments and let those stocks go, they will right away start to find their allocation. In time, one will double; another will lose half its value. You gave them a fair starting line, but wake up on day two and they won't be even any longer.

And shouldn't! The future happens. Truth will out: You will have made some fantastic picks, and some fantastically bad ones too. The passage of time will make it increasingly evident which is which, as your horses separate.

That perfect *balance* with which you started will become *imbalance*. And the conventional wisdom will then suggest you *rebalance*.

Not I. I say instead:

⋯→ ESTABLISH YOUR SLEEP NUMBER. ←⋯

Which takes some explanation.

BACK YOUR THOROUGHBREDS
AND RETIRE YOUR ALSO-RANS

You're already familiar with this basic idea: Water your flowers and cut your weeds. I spoke to it earlier in the book. Peter Lynch popularized it well in the 1980s, and if we looked hard enough we'd probably find it goes all the way back to the Greeks.[92]

Now, the minority of investors who *actually abide* by this practice probably think of it on a stock-by-stock basis. I'm here with Principle #4 to elevate it to an uber strategy that should run your portfolio.

The underlying notion is to reinforce success and minimize failure. Lynch's metaphor is perfect, really, but as it's also entered the realm of the threadbare, let's have a bit of Foolish fun and say the same thing using a selection of fresher metaphors:

Fuel your rockets and ground your anchors.
Feed your tigers and starve your snails.
Light your stars and dim your lanterns.
Build your castles and abandon your ruins.
Polish your gems and ignore your pebbles.

All very visual and some quite alluring!

But sticking to my Part III horse racing metaphor, I'll go with: **Back your thoroughbreds and retire your also-rans.** Which will so benefit you and your portfolios throughout your investing life. (Like much good investing advice, it works outside investing too; it works in business; it works in life.)

And yet if you pursue this principle long and far enough, you'll wind up courting extreme volatility in your portfolios, which will come to be dominated by the movements of a handful of stocks.

---

92 While the number of ancient texts speaking to stock market investors rounds to zero, Aristotle may have come closest when he emphasized the importance of practical wisdom (*phronesis*) and acting in accordance with our virtue. That includes knowing when to persist with what works (watering flowers) and when to abandon what doesn't (cutting weeds).

That's where your sleep number comes in.

PILLOW TALK ABOUT PORTFOLIO CONCENTRATION

You may recognize it: "Sleep number" is borrowed from the mattress industry.[93] Sleep Number mattresses allow you to set the firmness for your side of the bed using a number from 1 to 100, with higher numbers indicating firmer settings. This feature lets two sleeping partners each personalize their firmness on the same mattress.

I love the phrase "sleep number" for a different reason; it perfectly captures a key principle of Rule Breaker portfolios. Here's how we define it:

It's the highest percentage you'd allow any holding in your portfolio to reach, while still sleeping soundly at night.

It's a critical number to have in mind, and will guide you the rest of your way. There's no one-size-fits-all answer, and where you wind up says a lot about your risk tolerance, investment strategy, proximity to retirement, and financial goals. Establishing this number helps you manage your portfolio with confidence.

Let's take an example.

Let's start with a sleep number of five. A sleep number of five for investors means you are not comfortable having any more than 5% of your money in your largest holding. That sounds very much like an index fund to me and indeed most of the world, at least the portion of the world that owns index funds (a large portion), has a low-single-digit sleep number. Thanks to investments in funds like the trillion-dollar Vanguard Total Market Fund, these investors enjoy massive diversification with no single holding making much of a difference for good or ill. The largest companies in the world may be 5% positions, massive players like Microsoft and

---

93   ... from one of my worst-ever stock picks, in fact, ticker symbol SNBR. From my selection of it at $136 a share in February 2021 (at the height of the Covid-fueled market rise), it sat at $15 as of this writing. Down 89%.

Apple, but they're surrounded by thousands of other investments.[94] Again I say that if this is you, you're taking a very conservative approach, probably emphasizing predictability and capital preservation. Being clear on why you have such a low sleep number (and probably a large number of holdings) is the key. Again, there is no right or wrong or one-size-fits-all answer.

Now, an opposite example. How about a sleep number of 80? That means the investor sleeps soundly at night with their largest position being potentially four times the size of the rest of the portfolio combined! That is a really big, crazy-high number, but I use it because it was a number that I once rocked.

And thereby hangs a tale.

As I earlier mentioned, America Online was my first great stock. From my 1994 purchase price, AOL rose 150 times in value over the next six years. By now, you know me pretty well—I'm the guy who says things like, "Winners win!" and, "Let your winners run. High."[95] Even while following Principle #3, ensuring a fair starting line for your portfolio's investments, if one of those horses charges ahead and laps the field 150 times while some others are struggling to finish their first lap, you're going to end up with a *lot* in that stock.

For me at its maximum, AOL was right around 80% of my portfolio.

I was comfortable with that for three reasons. (I am giving out these reasons not to persuade you to imitate me, but simply to explain my own mindset and context.)

First, I'm comfortable with extreme volatility. I just am. I hate it when my stocks drop, of course, and if you're allocated this way you can lose a lot of your portfolio choking on a single morning's croissant. But I can take it (I know this about myself); you already know the "losing to win" mentality, and the math of it. I can take it largely because my stocks

---

94 For investors for whom even 5% of their money—a sleep number of five—is too much, there are "equal-weighted" funds that don't let any holding get above 1%.

95 Direct quote from the debut of Ye Olde Printed Foole, July 1993 issue: "The least mentioned, biggest risk of all is not taking enough risk."

possess the Six Traits, and probably most of all because the rewards to which my sleep number has led me are so much the greater.

Second, I was young—in my 20s.[96] This would very likely not be true of me in my 60s or 70s (not there yet). Your age factors in here—you have a lot more time for comebacks (and opportunities to learn), the younger you are.

Third and probably most important, as an entrepreneur my biggest holding is ownership in the business I helped found. It's both a luxury and a curse that so many other small business people can appreciate: Your own business is very likely the greatest source of your wealth. That fact alone has allowed me to take more risk in my equities portfolio than I would have, otherwise. That's why you see a lot of company founders, from the big dogs like Jeff Bezos down to us smaller fry, programmatically selling off bits and pieces of their company stock over the years. That comes from their wealth managers who are saying things like, "Hey, Jeff, you have over 90% of your fortune in one stock. That's crazy. You shouldn't have a sleep number that high. We, your wealth managers, would like you to reduce that over time," which is rational, well-intended, and good advice.

AOL, as everyone knows, didn't end well. Navigating its awkward Time Warner merger in a world that was shifting from dial-up to broadband, AOL wound up in a long-term decline from which it never recovered. My net worth certainly took a hit, but with new Rule Breakers popping up, I began systematically to reallocate elsewhere.[97]

I don't recommend a sleep number of 80 to anyone, and these days I'm closer to 35. Even a sleep number of 35 probably places me at the near edge of crazy. (Most people are probably comfortable with 10. The riskier-inclined would gravitate around 20.) And anyway, my point again is not to argue for any given number. It's to ensure you:

⋯⟶ ESTABLISH YOUR SLEEP NUMBER. ⟵⋯

---

96 Same decade I jumped out of a plane. Once. (Not planning on doing that again.) But there's probably some correlation between skydiving and sleep numbers.

97 Hello there, Netflix. 😌

Each of us is unique. Your age, risk tolerance, interest in this subject, amounts of money and of attention, all factor in. As I wrote earlier, it's for these reasons that Part III can only be suggestive... though in this chapter I suppose I *am* prescribing that you establish your sleep number. The number itself will always be your call, for reasons only you will fully understand.

And that sleep number will change too, over the course of your life! Has for me.

AGAINST REBALANCING

Many investment advisors and much of the regulated fund industry, when facing imbalance, *rebalance*. This is the practice of automatically selling positions that have risen, in order to reinvest the proceeds into those that have fallen. It enables various investment instruments to achieve their objective to remain well balanced across their holdings.

They can't help themselves; it's in their charter! Plus, it's conservative and sounds logical. But with your Rule Breaker jester-style thinking cap on, you start to see they're *backing their also-rans and retiring their thoroughbreds.* No wonder investment funds and advisors broadly underperform market averages.

Good news (more coming next chapter!): As an individual investor managing your own portfolio, you don't have to genuflect at the altar of Rebalance. You can use both your brain and intuition (some people call that horse sense).

Back your thoroughbreds and retire your also-rans.

A FEW FINAL CONSIDERATIONS

Some closing thoughts....

First, a single gigantic and widely diversified mutual fund can easily be 50% or more of your overall portfolio. You are technically invested in hundreds if not thousands of stocks, and your only risk would be if the fund somehow cratered for reasons that would be hard to foresee. I don't think someone heavily invested with their 401(k) in Vanguard's Total

Market or S&P 500 index funds needs to think too much about sleep numbers at all. Keep saving. Keep sleeping.

Second, if your portfolio is just starting and you don't right away have 20 stocks to give you 5% max initial position (Habit #5), that is okay. Especially if you don't have a broker who enables you to buy fractional shares. You should still get started investing, in the same spirit that my buying in thirds strategy says jump into the game right away with that first third, emphasizing action. Remember, the market tends to go up; getting started investing is the most valuable thing for newcomers.

So if you only have eight stocks and you're starting with a smaller amount of money, looking to save and build from there, you may have an elevated sleep number for some months. The key is to establish it up front and then work toward it, as needed. Some people make quite a lot in salary and are just starting their investing. If this is you and especially if the amounts you're investing are paltry compared to your paychecks, at this stage your sleep number doesn't count for much.

Third, I want to credit Paul Nourbash for writing in to the Rule Breaker Investing podcast mailbag with this thought: Maybe your sleep number should be set, in part, relative to *what kind of stock* is your largest holding. Paul gave an example. As a medical professional, he'd been attracted to my pick of Shockwave Medical (SWAV) because the company adapted ultrasonic technology originally used to treat kidney stones to instead begin treating heart disease—the number one killer in the U.S. From the pick in April 2019, Shockwave went on to rise 700%+, and for Paul it became his largest holding. "I purchased early, I watered my growing flowers, and in the end I had a position that was greater than my sleep number. Just as I started to feel like I might want to sell some shares and trim down the position, Johnson & Johnson purchased the company for $335 per share! My problem was solved: The cash is now in my account."

This fortunate timing relieved the stress he had been feeling with a smaller-cap company holding the top position in his portfolio. Paul noted that if it had been a mega-cap like Apple, he wouldn't have been concerned at all.

Now we're getting into nuances, which is exactly what each of us faces, as we're all in unique situations. But I like Paul's point and offer it for your consideration. The simplicity of a sleep number is part of its charm, but *for some, the* type *of stock filling that sleep number position* might make you view things differently.

Fourth and final, money used properly really does help extend your peace of mind and even your longevity. Turns out the same is true of sleep! **Studies keep coming out confirming and reconfirming the importance of sleep.** In fact, both managing your money well and getting good sleep are vital to a long, healthy life. Both count for so much.

Therefore:

··→ *ESTABLISH YOUR SLEEP NUMBER.* ←··

CHAPTER 17

YOU GET TO
INVEST FOR THE
WHOLE RACE!

C HEATING IS A word drenched in negativity—and for good reason. But in Chapter 8, championing sustainable competitive advantage (Trait #2), I drew on one of my favorite Seth Godin columns. Godin lionized companies that have so honed their competitive advantage that it looks like cheating.

Seen this way, cheating is a humorous pejorative for exploiting one's inherent advantages to win, whatever the context. It can evoke mischievous glee when we exploit a situation for our benefit in a way others haven't discovered—or can't replicate. Of course, this isn't actual cheating; we're not harming anyone or breaking laws. We're simply doing what our God-given talents or unique situations enables us to do.

Time for some more examples:

How about people who read fast and retain everything (I'm neither)? It's totally unfair that they breeze through homework in half the time, or read three times as many books in a year—*and* actually remember what they've read: Cheating! *Athletes with natural gifts?* People who can dunk a basketball? Cheating![98]

---

98 Dunking *was* cheating in college basketball from 1967–1976. The NCAA banned the dunk before the 1967–1968 season, citing injury concerns and a desire to reduce the advantage of taller players (like Lew Alcindor... Kareem Abdul-Jabbar).

But not all examples are about natural talent. What about situational advantages? The express lane for people with fewer items at the grocery store—they fly through, while I wait in my slow line? Cheating! Early birds who book trips ahead of time, snag the best seats or rooms, and even get early-bird discounts? Cheating!

But if you *can* read fast... if you can dunk... if you only grabbed eight items at Trader Joe's... or you planned your holiday trip months in advance... those rewards feel earned. It's really about making the most of your advantages.

Rule Breaker Investing itself is full of "cheating" examples, and by now you can rattle them off. Wait, you can spend *less* time investing and make *more* money? Cheating! You started saving and investing early, giving your compounding clock a 10-year head start? Cheating! You studied hard, got a job in an important, emerging industry that gave you early recognition of a top dog and first-mover, and landed a crazy low cost basis in a Rule Breaker stock? Cheating!

Or this: Someone bought a stock at $15, then sold it to you at a new high of $25—and so they bought low, and sold high—yet meanwhile you bought the stock from them at an all-time high, and just kept holding, and didn't sell (because... you have no sell discipline)—and then *you made far more money off the stock than they did?* Cheating!

You read this book, discovered all my best habits, traits, and principles, and have now reached page 194... when most people won't ever bother? Cheating!

And since you've made it this far, here's one more cheat—one of my favorites. Most people, when they risk money at the horse track, have to commit *before* the starting bell. But when investing in the stock market, Principle #5 (good news):

⇢ YOU GET TO INVEST FOR THE WHOLE RACE! ⇠

Cheating.

WHEN TO SELL

The world changes, and so do our companies. They surprise us to the upside and the downside. Take Zoom Video Communications, for example. It skyrocketed during the pandemic ($80 to $580), only then to drop all the way back down as the world reopened ($580 to $60).

Zoom Video Communications (ZM): January 2020–March 2023

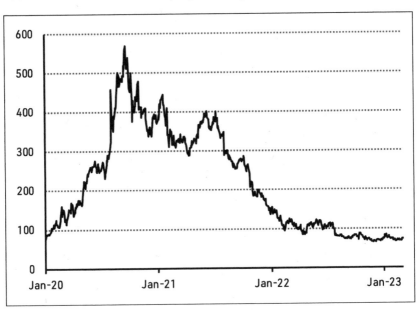

It's worth paying attention—at least quarterly, as I'll explain next chapter—because, as Principle #5 asserts, you get to invest for the whole race. That means taking advantage of the insights you gain year by year, furlong by furlong, to allocate your capital. Habit #2—adding up, *not* doubling down—has already conditioned you to back your thoroughbreds. Time for some words on retiring your also-rans.

By now you might be asking, "Should I never sell? Does David ever sell?" From our first book, *The Motley Fool Investment Guide*, I shared my simple sell rule, which I've stuck with ever since:

When you find a better place for your money, put it there.

And that's pretty much it for me. Other books may offer complex sell rules, impressing readers with their robust (sometimes contradictory) sell discipline. Fool that I am, I prefer to focus on what to buy (Part II), because *that's* where your most important decisions lie. When you buy well, you don't need a Harvard-endorsed sell discipline.

Still, my simple sell rule is worth remembering for those moments when you take a shine to something outside your portfolio more compelling than what's inside. That's why I frame it as a *portfolio-level* consideration. I don't recommend setting price targets on individual stocks; that approach often leads to over-trading. But at a high level, if you see horses outside your stable with better potential than the ones inside? *Now* we're talking (about selling)! If you find companies you esteem more than your current holdings, let me be the first to say: Always be upgrading.

I mostly sell to free up money for the stocks that better align with Principle #1: making your portfolio reflect your best vision for our future. If my portfolio is not fully reflecting that, selling can make sense.

You're free to bet on new horses entering mid-race (with unfair head starts)!

Freeing up money should come, foremost, from overweight positions exceeding your sleep number. If that's not an option, look to your losers, your also-rans. In the face of losing investments, many people hold on, hoping to get back to even; by contrast, I usually do the opposite. I'm always looking to sell off my losers, especially near year-end to offset capital gains for tax purposes. I've paid a lot in income taxes; I aim to minimize capital gains tax. Rule Breaker Investing, with its long-term holding focus, is a superlative way to grow wealth.

Now, if you don't have any overweight positions or good losers[99] to sell, but still want to always be upgrading, you'll face a tougher choice. Yet you already have a strong foundation to guide you: The six Rule Breaker stock traits. You're getting to invest the whole race, so as you're watching it, which of your existing companies no longer embodies these Six Traits in a way it once did, compared to the new stock you're eyeing? For me, that

---

99　Oxymoron alert.

often answers the question; I hope for you too. (If you're still undecided, the next chapter will introduce my Five-and-Three framework.)

Two final thoughts, both under the rubric: "Be Slow to Sell."

First, a classic quote often attributed to both Benjamin Graham and Warren Buffett: "The stock market was invented to move money from the impatient to the patient." While it's not literally true, it captures the system pretty well, if cynically. Impatient people who sell quickly do transfer their wealth over time to long-term shareholders of great companies. So, be slow to sell.[100]

Second, when it's not fear-driven, I think people (me included) want to feel really smart when they sell. Ha-ha, we think, I outsmarted the market; look how that stock, or the market overall, *dropped* soon after I sold. Some pundits have built their professional reputations on that one great call they made, selling just before everything hit the fan. But if you really want to feel *not* smart, look at the times you sold good stocks too early.

I once wrote a Motley Fool Stock Advisor column reviewing results over more than 10 years (146 consecutive monthly stock picks) and the numbers didn't lie: **We would have earned higher returns had I never sold a single stock.** The same was true for my brother Tom's 146 picks.

In October 2003, I recommended ARM Holdings, the UK-based intellectual property giant powering global innovation with its semiconductor designs. It traded at $4.75. Two months later, I re-recommended it ("add up") just under $6. We held those positions for five plus years, and...

... they dropped... to $3.27.

In June 2009, I put out my sell recommendation: "It's largely been a disappointment," I wrote dispiritedly. "We're selling it now because we believe the years ahead will bring more of the same." They didn't. In 2016, Softbank bought out the company at $22.50.

In that same writeup, I had noted separately that we'd successfully

---

100 Let traders chase trendy, short-term lists of hot stocks—like the "Magnificent Seven." Being slow to sell means giving your best stocks the time they need to become *truly* magnificent. Rule Breaker investors do better instead to maximize our "Magnificent Seven score" (cf. Glossary!).

sold a shaggy dog of a loser (Strayer Education), which had gone on to lose another 75% since we'd sold. We probably felt pretty smart there! But trading out of home run stocks like ARM, even alongside some timely sells, is tough to recover from. The math works greatly against you.[101] See for yourself by tracking your own performance; I bet you, like me, will find that selling great stocks "loses" more money through opportunity cost than we ever lose on our bad stocks.

So, if you find a better place for your money, put it there. But be slow to sell.

INVESTING VS. SPORTS BETTING

As I wrote earlier in Part III, these principles are suggestive, not prescriptive, given everyone's unique situation, resources, and mindset. The key to Principle #5 is simple: Use what's happening in the race to make every additional investment you make, *during the race*, smarter. This is in contrast to a raging new area of speculation in this era: sports betting, to which I briefly want to speak.

Sports betting, of course, is all-or-nothing, and the bet has to be put down before the game is played.

Sports bettors have numerous disadvantages compared to stock market investors. They routinely have to take all-or-nothing propositions, pay an intermediary ("the House") up to 10% commission, and have to put down all their money *before* the race, the game, starts. It's regrettable how easy and attractive sports betting is made to sound, when it's such a losing play, day in and day out. I'm hoping this book reaches many and helps clarify for them why their money is so much better invested in the stock market.

The market tends to rise over time (you and me in the sailboat, the wind at our backs); sports betting by its nature is zero-sum, and your expected return is always negative. The handicaps are set very effectively

---

101   ARM had gained 588% from our sale. Strayer had dropped -75% from our sale. Average those out and it's quite an opportunity cost. We'd need about six more "great" sales of dog stocks like Strayer to equal out the mistake of selling one position of ARM. And we had two.

(whether we're talking about a 6.5-point favorite in basketball or 7–5 odds at a horse track). One bettor will win, the other will lose, and the House will always take its cut. **Over time, almost all consistent sports bettors lose money.**

What happens to those who consistently invest over time?

The difference is immense. Though sports betting is now widely legal in the U.S., that doesn't make it a smart bet. I've made friendly wagers with friends for decades, which can make watching games more fun (and stressful). But I look askance at big-volume betting, and especially its influence on the media coverage of sports I love. A booming gambling industry does not reflect my best vision for our future.

Sports betting, as has been said of state lotteries, functions broadly as yet another tax on imbeciles. While some bettors may see it differently, the reality is that over time, most will lose their money.

ARE YOU AN INVESTOR, OR A SUNSHINE PATRIOT?

Picturing handsome steeds, proud jockeys, and all this colorful talk of winning is inspiring, and rightly so. Principle #5 is a hand-clapping encouragement:

··→ YOU GET TO INVEST FOR THE WHOLE RACE! ←··

Yet, a closing word for the wise: Never forget that, repeatedly at different points throughout the race, things will look bad or even bleak.

Throughout this whole race, the market will drop, *lose* value, one year in three. And your money with it—and in my experience, Rule Breaker investors often get hit hardest during downturns. No coincidence I gave up on ARM Holdings in 2009; unless you were born before 1932, you've never seen a worse year for the Dow Jones Industrial Average (2008: -33.8%—the Nasdaq Composite was -40.5%).[102]

Getting to invest through the whole race is a privilege and a pain. Prepare for recurrent losing, self-doubt, maybe tears. I've experienced all three. So, some encouragement for when you need it:

Thomas Paine (1737–1809) was the American Revolutionary War pamphleteer and author of *Common Sense* who brought tremendous eloquence to the cause for American freedom (despite himself being born British). His famous and most timeless line speaks to you and me at every dark turn: *These are the times that try men's souls.*

But while many Americans may recognize that line above, and might even know it's Thomas Paine, fewer will remember what follows:

These are the times that try men's souls: The summer soldier and the sunshine patriot will, in this crisis, shrink from the service of their country; but he that stands it now, deserves the love and thanks of man and woman. Tyranny, like Hell, is not easily conquered; yet we have this consolation with us, that the harder the conflict, the more glorious the triumph. What we obtain too cheap, we esteem too lightly: It is dearness only that gives every thing its value.

That image of the summer soldier and the sunshine patriot—a glowing reminder of Paine's gift for the *mot juste*—never fails to stir my imagination.

It was written for the War for American Independence, of course. But as both an American and a lifelong stock market enthusiast, I highlight this passage to help inspire my fellow Rule Breakers as we endure every Great Bear Market. Look again at the quotation, and just substitute a few words (e.g., for "service of their country" put in "stock market"). One can very easily see how Thomas Paine was, across time, speaking to investors today.

---

102   Shocking volatility, too. In the 56 trading days that followed September 15, 2008, fully 26 of them featured market moves of 4% or greater. In the preceding 25 years, there had been only 29 such days!

The world is every bit as full now as it may have been then of summer soldiers and sunshine patriots. They buy stock in happy times, or at least talk about it at cocktail parties. How long they hold those shares is less clear; many flee at the first sign of trouble (and yes, they might have saved capital in 2008 by doing so). But they will all come to sell their shares, many at the worst time—the very bottom, right when they should be buying. They sell to their opposites, to the winter soldier and the patient patriot. To you and me, if we're buying.

At a Motley Fool event in November 2008, during the market plunge, I asked over 200 people in the room for a show of hands: How many had bought a stock in the past 60 days? Though my own portfolio was down over 40%, I raised my hand. But I wasn't the only one: Approximately 200 other hands went up, too. I realized that night that I was among winter soldiers.

Though we couldn't know it at the time, those fall purchases would become some of the best we would ever make.

It isn't easy being a winter soldier. It doesn't feel fun at all. Investors get no instant gratification. When, wreathed in gloom, you send in your order to buy, you won't know for at least three years if you made the right choice.

As Thomas Paine once wrote, *the harder the conflict, the more glorious the triumph*. His words celebrated here were read to the soldiers of General George Washington, at Washington's order, to keep their spirits up as they prepared for the Battle of Trenton.

Remember them in your every winter.

CHAPTER 18

REVIEW QUARTERLY, MANAGE ACCORDINGLY

"Il faut cultiver notre jardin."

—VOLTAIRE,
CANDIDE, OU L'OPTIMISME

N O MATTER HOW many stocks are in your portfolio, the frequency and amount of attention you give them can be the same. Outrageous premise, right? I'm saying whether you have 20 stocks, around 60 (like me), or 100+, the frequency and focus of your check-ins need not differ.

The check-in frequency itself, I've already given you. It's up there in lights, in the chapter's title. Principle #6:

··→ **REVIEW QUARTERLY, MANAGE ACCORDINGLY.** ←··

I follow the market daily, just as I follow my sports teams daily. I love seeing the games of investing or baseball play out, who's scoring and how. I also keep up with other teams and stocks that are not mine. It's the action I love, and staying informed. Some (you?) feel that following the market day-by-day might lead to over-trading. They may be right, and so discipline is key. But I'm not going to trade away my stocks—or favorite teams—just because I watch the Nasdaq or check every box score. For me, more attention deepens my appreciation. Like life.

In terms of a review—formal or not—taking time to reflect every three months on your portfolio, yourself, and the world feels about right. It's enough time to see meaningful changes, like a great earnings report or a 25% haircut, but not so much time that you're missing the big picture. Remember, you get to invest the whole race! Checking in quarterly will be rewarding, whether for tweaks, trades, or that final third you're ready to buy.

Oh, and if you're *slammed* for a given quarter and can't find time, don't worry—this book and Rule Breaker Investing have your back. We're the opposite of the flash-trade brigade. Your portfolio already reflects your best vision for our future. Your stocks and the market will still be there, when you're ready.

Now, the actual time you choose to give your portfolio is up to you. Maybe it's five hours a quarter, maybe 50. This depends on your degree of interest, the time you have, and your priorities. The good news? Whatever time you give, it works the same whether you own 10 stocks or 100.

A QUICK GUIDE TO RULE BREAKER TIME MANAGEMENT

The trick is to group your holdings, and follow accordingly.

For stocks representing more than 5% of your portfolio, spend *extra time*. Review quarterly earnings, check out conference calls, monitor industry trends, and evaluate analyst reports. Aim to know more about this company than most people you'd ever casually bump into (other than maybe Sally). Extra time is worthily spent here—these few stocks (there won't be more than a few) really count!

For stocks in the 1.5%–5% range, let's call that *regular time*. Regular time will reflect your tastes and modus operandi. For most, scanning key news headlines since the last review does the trick. Again, if you're keeping up weekly (or day-to-day, like the fanboy that I am) you may already know this stuff. Regular time, for you, might include following online discussions, or management interviews on YouTube. I've used Motley Fool CAPS (caps.fool.com) over the years to great effect for community intelligence. Maybe you're in an investing club, sharing intel with others. Does this sound onerous? Don't let it be. Here's an AI prompt (tweak away; make it your own):

> I'm doing a three-month review for the following stock(s)....
> Highlight any key stories a shareholder should know. Keep the response to 250 words, provide links out, focused on the most important updates.

Works for me.[103]

For stocks that account for less than 1.5%, feel free to give them *down time.* Am I saying not to follow them? No—but if something has to give, let it be this group. The ones that do well will reach higher allocations, and the ones that don't—well, would pouring your heart into them have helped? (Though, if you bought a starter position because the company fascinates you, follow that fascination!)

Whether you have 20 positions or 200, this approach helps you focus your time in more impactful ways, regardless of your stock count.

And how's this for a Foolishly contrary conclusion: **You can spend less time following your portfolio, the more stocks you own.** Read that again. Think about it. Another great argument for diversification.

LEVEL UP: THE FIVE-AND-THREE FRAMEWORK

Last chapter, in discussing when to sell, I noted that it's not always as simple as trimming a position back to your sleep number, or dumping a

---

103   This prompt example will soon look simplistic and outdated. As a lifelong fan of emerging technologies, I'm acutely aware that our present-day AIs (which still get some things wrong—and need to be double-checked!) will get progressively better, and easier to use. Pick your poison.

loser to zero out a capital gain. Sometimes, your quarterly review asks a tougher question: What will you sell to buy that new stock you're excited about, or to fund a down payment on a home (why we invest in the first place!)? If you want to keep things simple, you can raise the needed cash by selling a uniform percentage portion of a basket of positions (say, 10% of each), though that might complicate your taxes.

For more serious investors looking to level up, I want to share my framework to help with sell decisions. It's all about asking future-focused questions and setting expectations. Because, check it, all that matters for our investment returns is what happens *next*. Yesterday's news and yesterday's moves are already priced in. By clearly stating your expectations for key holdings and scoring them over time, you'll be in a much smarter position to make decisions. When I picked stocks for The Motley Fool, we used a Five-and-Three for every selection: five green flags, three red flags (yes, racing language keeps popping up in Part III).

First, what are five key things you're looking for to go right? I call them green flags. These are five bullish signs you're watching for. Green flags exist to confirm your original rationale for buying, your *thesis*, is still holding true. And on the flip side, what are three things that could go wrong? Three red flags to acknowledge in a kind of *pre-mortem*—bad signs that, if they start showing up, might signal it's time to consider selling.

This framework flags what really drives stock performance: future developments. It doesn't need to be intense—spend as much or as little time as you want, based on how important the holding is for you.

Here's an example. I'll name the company and the year shortly, but first, let's look at how it worked:

5 Green Flags

1. The Z Corp. acquisition brings even better revenue growth, particularly in architectural and automotive prototyping.
2. Cubify.com gains critical mass, helping sales of the Cube consumer 3-D printer overtake popular rival MakerBot.
3. An uptick in print materials sold (the consumable resins, etc., its parts are printed from) boosts margins.

4. The company continues to add new offerings of print materials to its catalog.

5. The acquisition of Vidar advances 3D's leadership in health care.

3 Red Flags

1. Organic growth can't hold on to its first-quarter improvements.

2. Net and operating margins both decline.

3. The newly combined Stratasys and Objet Geometries cut into 3D's vertical markets.

Taking time to visualize a stock's future isn't for every investor, but even a small effort gives you a roadmap to follow. Five-and-Threes can be built anytime, updated as needed, and provide excellent fodder for quarterly reviews. And while I have contextualized it here to speak to selling, a company hitting all its green flags (maybe even greener than you foresaw!) may draw your attention the other direction: Maybe one to move from your watchlist to your buy list. Or, if you already own it, add up (*don't* double down).

Speaking of not doubling down, I'm glad we never did that for 3D Systems, whose 2012 Five-and-Three I shared above. (Give yourself a gold star if you recognized the company—and if you've been a shareholder, that virtual gold star may be all you're getting out of $DDD....) I first recommended the stock for Motley Fool Stock Advisor in January 2012 at $12, added more six months later in the $20s, and by January 2014 it crossed $90. Two years later, it fell below $10. We sold in November 2020 at $6.[104]

I wouldn't be a true Fool if I didn't share the losses as well as the wins. Our initial Five-and-Three gave generally good signals in the near term, and in a way that makes sense since the stock was a 7+-bagger (briefly) in its first two years! But if you look at it since those red flags,

---

104 History will show that just months later it got an unbelievable "Covid pop" from $6 up over $50(!), back down to $10 in 2021, and at $3 as of this writing.

especially around profit margin, came true. I wish I'd paid more attention, or updated it more often. Lessons learned.

Oh, by the way, why does this framework feature five green and only three red flags? Why not five and five, or two green and 10 red?

Rule Breaker Investing works in part because we take a positive view of the world, while others focus on faults, fears, and trying to protect against the downside. Which is why I often ask: What if things go right? *What if they go really right?* If you're considering becoming part owner of a company via the miracle of the stock market, aren't you seeking more bullish signs than bearish ones?

MANAGE ACCORDINGLY

There's something pleasingly positive yet open-ended about the phrase "manage accordingly," in line with the spirit of Part III. Managing is what we do every day—our time, relationships, health, and yes, I'm a big fan of managing our own money, too. **No one cares more about your money than you.** Managing your own portfolio has a choose-your-own-adventure feel, like those interactive books you may have enjoyed as a child.

So when I say at the end here, "manage accordingly," I hope it clicks. First, manage your Six Habits to excellence. Then, manage your stock picks—companies of which you're proud to be a part owner—guided by the Six Traits. Thus, if you are practicing these habits and seeking these traits, what results is a portfolio, *your portfolio*, that can stand strong on Six Principles, those to get started (Principles #1–#3) and to sustain (Principles #4–#6). And so "manage accordingly" means staying adaptable, staying engaged, and ultimately trusting yourself to navigate the ups and downs with confidence. These Habits, Traits, and Principles form the foundation—how you choose to build on them is entirely up to you.

Indeed, habits are but mindsets; traits, observations that you spy out. Together, they exist to support you as aiders and abettors, in the same way that Tolkien's Fellowship of the Ring existed, briefly and bravely, ultimately just to get Frodo and Sam to Mount Doom. It was up to the *actions taken* by those two hobbits to save their world.

And for you, aided by habits and traits, it is now for you to convert their potential energy into the kinetic energy and pure action of building and growing your portfolio.

You're on your own, now. You now know all my best thoughts. So, choose your own adventure! And as you proceed:

··→ REVIEW QUARTERLY, MANAGE ACCORDINGLY. ←··

At the end of his landmark work *Candide*, Voltaire offers a timeless reminder. In five words, he tells us that while we can't control what happens in the world at large, we can shape our own circumstances. The hero, Candide, has been through a long series of adventures filled with hardship and disillusionment. At the conclusion, he has an exchange with his neighbor, a Turkish farmer, who explains that he and his family lead a simple, fulfilling life by working hard and avoiding involvement in the grander, often chaotic affairs of the world. It's in this context that Candide delivers the final line: *Il faut cultiver notre jardin*—we must cultivate our garden.

And so, at the end of Part III:

With an eye on the future, with clear-eyed purpose, your own "right" number of stocks, good sleep at night, and the freedom to invest the whole race... manage accordingly.

Cultivate your garden.

THE 6 PRINCIPLES OF THE RULE BREAKER PORTFOLIO

PRINCIPLE #1:
MAKE YOUR PORTFOLIO REFLECT YOUR BEST VISION FOR OUR FUTURE.

PRINCIPLE #2:
KNOW AND NAME ITS PURPOSE.

PRINCIPLE #3:
FAIR STARTING LINE.

PRINCIPLE #4:
ESTABLISH YOUR SLEEP NUMBER.

PRINCIPLE #5:
YOU GET TO INVEST THE WHOLE RACE!

PRINCIPLE #6:
REVIEW QUARTERLY, MANAGE ACCORDINGLY.

I SET OUT TO write a book whose every chapter might be its own lesson. **Follow any lesson—read any single chapter—and I believe you'll be smarter, happier, and richer.** Yet here *you* are, having made it all the way through, and so now you know something more: Each Habit, Trait, and Principle works together, creating force multipliers.

Use what you like among these to build something beautiful— something that, for me, has been invaluable. It's made me laugh and cry, put my kids through school, put a roof over our heads, put The Motley Fool on the map. It's something I hope you'll embrace, cherish, something that will take you—up a rollercoaster!—to the Land of the Free.

Your portfolio.

It does not come cheap. Yet the harder the conflict—*there will be so many more market drops*—the more glorious the triumph. What we obtain too cheap, we esteem too lightly: It is dearness only that gives every thing its value.

SUMMARY OF PART III: TALE OF TWO INVESTORS

Sally picked up the phone. "Hello, Mr. Soros. Yes, I understand your concerns about the project timeline. Uh-huh... yes, bifacials *are* more expensive. It's not unusual for these things to come in a little late and a little over budget.

"Okay, I get it. I understand your concerns, sir... yet I hope you'll still invest! This needs to be a win for everyone—the tortoises too. Thanks for considering!"

Clara picked up right away on what Sally had just done there. "You are still cultivating more investors?"

"A-B-U, Clara. Always be upgrading."

"Speaking of upgrading," Clara countered, "I have just the little upgrade for you and your coffee date, Saturday...! You two connected over investing, right?"

"Right."

"Here's a fun idea—I got this idea from a friend. Each of you should show up in a T-shirt—of a stock you own! Y'know, like a company T-shirt. Extra points for cheesy corporate taglines."

"That's pretty hilarious...."

Sally wasn't hard to pick out at the Starbucks that Saturday. Harry had already liked the look of her, but today she seemed even more put together. Maybe the deep green of her T-shirt brought out her eyes? He smirked, glancing down at the logo.

"Nvidia, huh?"

Sally extended her arms with a smile and a flourish. "Powering the future of AI," she mused, reading aloud the front. She took a bow. "I've owned this one for a long time, since 2005 actually! When I joined this newslett—oh, but anyway, what's yours?"

If her shirt was shiny, his was... shabby.

"Yeah... well, I liked your silly idea," Harry replied, seeing her look down at his chest. "You don't know this company?" She didn't. "I got the stock from some old newsletter service I canceled years ago. It's 3D Systems."

"'Printing the Future,' eh?" Sally read. "Is that 3-D printing?"

"Something like that. I was thinking of adding more here—stock's down below $3." Did Sally just frown? "My trading app was offering me a discount and an avatar upgrade, if I pulled the trigger."

"Avatar upgrade?"

"For fun. Gamifying? I'd unlock a new costume..."

"... of?"

"But I didn't." Harry walked with her to the counter. Caffeine. Good. He hadn't slept well last night. "So, what's your poison?"

While waiting for their drinks, Sally mentioned she led a women's investment club, the InvestHers. "Do you like the name?" He chuckled. "Nvidia's in our portfolio, but it's causing some first-world problems. We keep selling it down, to help the ladies sleep at night!" She was obviously proud of her crew. "Our club's higher purpose is to empower women through education, so we channel some of our gains into financial literacy programs for women and girls who need it most."

Okay, Harry was impressed. That said, he was also fast realizing there were no good seats. This place was packed, at lunch!

His watch buzzed—a text from Jake.

hey harry, got something for you
you guys at SBUX downtown?
bounce two blocks down my way
join me

Jake was always a card. Harry texted back, asking where—and whether he had two warm seats.

horse track, and yeah—feature race, 20 minutes

Sally had been to a derby as a little girl, but it didn't have the grandeur and energy of today's race track, which felt electric. The crowd's buzz mixed with the distant neighing of horses, the smell of fresh popcorn, and the bright colors of jockey silks flashing like confetti in the afternoon sun.

True to his word, Jake had found two extra prime seats in a cozy box overlooking the track. "How are you two *stock*birds? Wait, Harry: You wore *that*?" Harry stuck out his tongue. "Anyway, feature race is in... six minutes." Jake glanced at the tote board. "Get your bets down, lady and gentleman."

Harry handed Sally 25 bucks.

"Wha-?"

"Twenty-five for you, 25 for me," Harry beamed.

"Harry does things like this all the time at the office. He's bought me more drinks than I've bought for myself."

"But how do we... what do we bet on?" Sally looked out of her element.

Harry smirked. "You could bet on the horse with the fanciest name. Or the one that looks like it had a good night's sleep."

Jake chimed in. "Or my strategy: longest odds, shortest legs. Always a winner." He pushed the program toward her so she could give the field of contenders a once-over. "Oh, and I got one rule to spice things up," Jake went on. "You each place your $25 bet... but, *secretly*. No telling who you picked, till the end."

Back minutes later from the betting window, they took their seats. But Harry wasn't done; he had one last trick up his sleeve. "Okay, Sally, you ready? You made your bet. I made mine. And Jake made us not squeal. So here's the final twist."

And he handed her his betting slip, face down. Sally paused, puzzled.

"It's a gift, Tortoise Shell! I'm giving you the gift of my insight. You've got my bet."

Sally was surprised again, and surprisingly touched. "Okay then, fella... I didn't know day traders disguised as data marketing analysts could be so *charming*." She nudged her own betting slip face down toward him. "Happy first date. Hope it's a winner."

And they're off.

At the track bar late that afternoon, The Winner's Circle, Jake bade them adieu. "And you two still won't reveal what you bet on? Geez, stockbirds keep their secrets." Harry and Sally grinned, thanking him for hosting. "Well, if either of you did actually win anything, the betting windows stay open for payouts until seven." He paused, hoping they'd relent; no luck. "Fine, fine... but Harry, I expect a full report Monday!"

As The Winner's Circle thinned out, it was time for The Reveal.

"Okay, you first," Sally said. "Go on, take a look."

Harry carefully turned over the betting slip she'd given him, handling it with care, like a Wonka golden ticket—which for him in some ways it was.

"Wonka-tastic.... So, what did she have for me?"

It was the #13 horse, Dashing Charm.

Sally blushed.

"Um, I don't exactly remember the track announcer calling 'Thirteen' much, down the stretch," Harry teased. "Like... zero times?"

Sally blushed again, this time with regret. "You said pick a name I liked, and he reminded me of someone. So I went with it! Then came the starting bell. He stumbled out of the gates, and finished... last. Sorry I lost you your 25 dollars."

Harry kept looking at the ticket. "Dashing Charm, huh?" Sally blushed a third time. "Okay, time for you to open my gift."

"What'd you get me...?" Sally pulled out her own golden ticket, turning it over. "Oh my gosh! No way, no... *WAY!*"

"I guess I've got a good eye for winners?" he said, fixing on her. "Eh, Tortoise Shell?"

"Number Six horse for the win?" Sally was beside herself. "Twenty-five dollars times ten-to-one... that's 250 bucks!"

"Keep the change."

"But it's your money."

"And my gift to give."

"I had no idea who actually won! I was too busy watching Dashing Charm go backwards."

"Well, Number Six won easy. Truth be told, I don't know much about horse racing either. That's Jake's game. I just liked the name."

"Cultivate Your Garden?"

"And *down the stretch* they come," Harry imitated the race caller. "It's a one-horse race. Cultivate Your Garden! Cultivate Your Garden. It's Cultivate— ... *Cultivate Your Garden!* For the win!"

"You liked the name?"

"Made me think of you."

"Last call," said the bartender.

"Well, seeing as how I'm now flush with cash, how about I treat you to a drink, Harry?"

"Sure."

"Bartender, what's the signature cocktail tonight?"

"No problem, ma'am. Signature drink tonight is spiffy stuff... *and it's gonna pop*. Because it's something new: The Spiffy-Pop. Feelin' spiffy?"

"I'm into that," Sally chimed.

"And you?" the bartender glanced at Harry. "The fine lady's paying."

Harry looked from the bartender, to Sally, back to the bartender, and paused for one extra moment.

"I'll have what she's having."

CHAPTER X

EXCELSIOR

JEFF BEZOS WAS coming to my home city in the fall of 2018, to speak at The Economic Club of Washington D.C., and I planned to attend. It wasn't every day the richest man on the planet came to town. The event was sure to be a who's who of business, politics, and culture—it was going to be a bash.

I told my wife Margaret the day before, "If I ever get to the man, if I can catch up to him, here's my line. I'm gonna say, 'Jeff, I believe I'm the guy in the room with the *second* lowest cost basis on Amazon stock.'"

The guy with the lowest was the founder, Jeff Bezos himself. But for The Motley Fool and our members over the years, I wanted him to know I had picked Amazon shortly after its IPO at what was, for me, the now-iconic price of 16 cents. Even though the day I bought was many years before, most at the event would still have known Amazon back then—yet they'd likely have dismissed it as *just an overvalued online bookseller.*

I wanted to reconnect with Jeff, give him my line.

If I could get to him.

Because, though I'd interviewed Jeff before, that had been 20 years ago. It had been a lot easier to get him on The Motley Fool Radio Show back when Amazon was 1/100th of its size today.

In twilight the next evening I approached the Washington Hilton, surrounded by business *glitterati*, media officials, and security. Thousands were lining up. It was a circus, made louder by people across the street shouting over a loudspeaker, "Hell, no! Bezos has to go! Underpaying his workers." (This was before Amazon's minimum wage rose to $15.00 an hour.

Separately, that morning Bezos had announced a $2 billion Day One Fund to support homeless families and enhance early childhood education.)

I eventually managed—no small feat—to get inside the hotel lobby. I tried to get to the bar for a glass of wine. No dice. There were so many people—wasn't this place governed by fire code regulations?—*so* many people, elbow-to-elbow, it felt comic. I half-expected a clown car to pull up and unload a few more.

I began to realize: "... okay, I'm *not* going to be getting to Bezos tonight."

Reaching the welcome desk, I picked up the envelope with my seat assignment: Table 334. Now, I hadn't expected Table 1, but wow. *They were counting by ones....* Table 334 was a *long* way from the stage.

The event kicked off with David Rubinstein, the billionaire head of The Economic Club of Washington (ECW), as our emcee. Rubinstein is as generous as he is brilliant (and now—the principal owner of The Baltimore Orioles baseball team). He rattled off the long list of sponsors, then the names for scholarships the ECW was awarding. Oh, and: "Jeff Bezos is here tonight!" he announced, asking Bezos to stand up and wave. You could see, *way* up there in the front, a small hand wave, confirming that the man himself was in the room, ready for an interview over supper.

Finally, the 20 minutes of announcements wrapped as the salads appeared, signaling the start of dinner.

Except I had other plans.

I turned to the two gentlemen beside me, strangers all at Table 334: "Guys, I'm *going* for it. We'll all know, within five minutes, whether this works or not. I'm going to try to get to Bezos right now. Excuse me."

"Something has happened over the last decade in America," wrote pollster Mark Penn in *Microtrends Squared* (2018). "The most optimistic, can-do country has become mired in endless pessimism and negativity."

This shift is surprising—and deeply regrettable. I am firmly in the "Henry Ford Optimism School" (my phrase—I don't think this ever formally existed). Ford, born in 1863 during the worst period in U.S. history, revolutionized industry and made automobiles accessible to the masses. He's reputed to have said, **"Whether you think you can, or whether you think you cannot, you're right."**

Can I get an amen?

I've seen the power of optimism firsthand, especially with early-stage enterprises (including my own). The people who say, "Yes, we can," have exponentially more potential to succeed than those who say, "No, we cannot." It's no mere state of mind: Optimism is a creative force. *Do you believe you can buy and hold your way to a 100-bagger?* After this book, I sure hope so. I think you can. And if *you* think you can, you're vastly more likely to achieve it than if you think you cannot.

Jeff Bezos could have been a "no-can-do" person. Born to a teenage mother in Albuquerque, New Mexico, he faced considerable challenges, starting with his parents separating shortly after his birth. Raised by his mother and stepfather (a Cuban immigrant), Bezos's early life could easily have landed him, as Vin Scully might say, in the graveyard of broken dreams. It's not hard to see how he could have become an American "mired in endless pessimism and negativity."

But the greatest internet entrepreneur of this age had a different mindset:

'One of the only ways to get out of a tight box is to invent your way out.'

'I knew that if I failed, I wouldn't regret that, but I knew the one thing I might regret is not trying.'

'Always lean into the future... when the world changes around you and when it changes against you... you have to lean into that and figure out what to do... complaining isn't a strategy.'

'In the end, we are our choices. Build yourself a great story.'

And it's not just Bezos.

Long before founding Starbucks, Howard Schultz grew up in a public housing project in Brooklyn, New York.

Oprah Winfrey was born into poverty in rural Mississippi and faced numerous challenges during her childhood, including abuse. Today, she stands among the most influential media moguls in the world.

Jan Koum immigrated to the United States from Ukraine at the age of

16, living off food stamps and working as a cleaner to make ends meet. He later co-founded WhatsApp, which was acquired by Facebook (now Meta Platforms) for $19 billion.

And Steve Jobs, co-founder of Apple, was born to a young, unwed graduate student and put up for adoption. Raised by working-class parents, he later dropped out of college due to financial difficulties that had him sleeping on the floor of his friends' dorm rooms and collecting Coke bottles for money.

The rest, as they say, is history.

Except it's not that easy. It never is. Not one of these people had a head start. History could have no expectation any of them would make a mark. But:

In the end, we are our choices. Build yourself a great story.

I wasn't raised with a silver spoon in my mouth, though my parents did keep one with my name on it in a cupboard. That's my way of saying I came from a well-to-do family that didn't flaunt it.

Life wasn't always easy (it simply isn't, no such thing), but being raised in a two-parent household already put me points-up on the scoreboard. Both my grandfathers were successful entrepreneurs—one even owned a stake in a Major League Baseball team. My mother, the product of Irish Catholic families (Alabama and upstate New York), was the family Rule Breaker—as much as one could be as a society woman. My father was a Harvard-educated lawyer and, as I've mentioned before, he's the one who taught me to invest. At 18, I received from him my stock portfolio, which he had brilliantly invested for me since birth. I could have paid for college myself, but I got a full scholarship.

So I had nothing heroic to "overcome" to be at the Washington Hilton that night.

But aside from a low cost basis in Amazon, I did have one other thing clearly in common with Bezos and the other heroes I've mentioned. Maybe you have it too. For most of U.S. history, it has been broadly shared

Chapter X

both by landed families and immigrants alike, and is most clearly felt and communicated today by first-generation Americans:

I had Optimism.

Like many—especially in the business world—I proceed from a few core assumptions: I can do this; effort will be rewarded; you either win or you learn; and, you miss 100% of the shots you don't take (including 100% of the CEOs you don't buttonhole).

Whether you think you can, or whether you think you cannot, you're right.

Or, as Harry Truman famously said: "A pessimist is one who makes difficulties of his opportunities, and an optimist is one who makes opportunities of his difficulties."

Earlier, I said I hope you share this mindset. But if you don't, I hope you're closer to it *now*, here in Chapter X, than you were at the start of Chapter O. Who you are influenced by—who we read, for instance—determines so much of who we become.

I have a friend whose father-in-law, a wise old judge in Maryland's juvenile court, would give a talk to kids preparing to reenter the free world after detention:

"I can already tell you right now which of you will be back here [in jail] to see me again, and which of you won't," he would say. "It's simple: *Show me your friends.*"

We *are* our choices, including who we spend time with! "When you choose your friends today," James Clear writes, "you are choosing your habits tomorrow." Want to lose weight? Hang out with people who are losing weight. Want to be better with money? Spend time with people who save more than they spend. And if you want to see the bright side of life, surround yourself with people who radiate positivity and intelligence.

Here's a great line, shared with me by my friend Bill Burke, head of

The Optimism Institute,[105] though he's quoting Kevin Kelly, the rational optimist who co-founded *Wired*:

> **If you read today's headlines, you'll conclude things have never been worse. But if you read history, you'll conclude things have never been better.**

I got up from the table, made my way past Tables 330 and 329. Found my path into the high 200s. Wheeled around those, moved into the 100s... and then, decidedly, toward Table 1. (I thought: *What's the worst that could happen here?*) Now arriving at the front of the room, I took a look back at all the little tables—like Table 334—scattered thickly around the room like lily pads on a pond.

People were already starting supper.

But up here at the mountain top, the crowd was still standing and milling about, not yet seated. And there was Bezos, with just one guy talking to him.

This was it: I went and stood right behind that gentleman, half-listening to their conversation, which wound down after another two minutes. The guy stepped away. And there was Jeff.

For decades at The Motley Fool, one core value stands above the rest: your "motley," the value you—yes, *you*—bring to work every day. In a word or a phrase, it's what you most care about, what you aspire to, what defines you. It's how you choose to tell your story.

"What's your motley?" is our catchphrase. You can ask any of our 400+ employees and they'll have an answer. They work at a company where

---

105   www.theoptimisminstitute.com

their voice counts. Our most essential core value, the one that bears our name, asks: "Who are you, and what do you care about?" I've always said we are like a stained-glass window, with each new employee adding a piece of glass—with its own unique shape, its own alluring color.

Some of our employees take their motley deeply to heart, and can break yours with a 30-second story. Others have fun with theirs, hold it lightly, and change it often, like a flavor of the month.

(What's *your* motley?)

Mine has been the same from Day One, and I don't expect it to change. In Latin, it means, "Ever higher."

Excelsior.

Because I want the stock market to go ever higher. (And it does. Just give it time.) I've watched our business go ever higher, from the tiniest, humblest roots. I want the lives, the consciousness, the experiences of everyone around me—family, friends, my *Rule Breaker Investing* readers— to rise, too. I want to lift up everything around me, to see everything rise.

Excelsior always reminds me of excellence, too:

I try to find excellence, buy excellence, and add to excellence over time. I sell mediocrity. That's how I invest.

I looked him right in the eye, smiled, and said, **"Jeff, I believe I'm the guy in the room with the second lowest cost basis on Amazon stock."** Then: "Hi, Jeff. Great to see you again! David Gardner from The Motley Fool. I used to talk to you—"

And what did Bezos do?

He instantly replied, warmly and familiarly, "David!" Then he pulls his phone out of his pocket, puts his arm around me, holds the phone up. "Selfie!" he says.

And that's how I ended up in a selfie with Jeff Bezos.

A selfie I don't think I'll ever see, buried somewhere years deep on Jeff's phone!

But if I had to caption it, I'd go with: *L'Optimisme.* Two optimists from very different places... one with a company a *lot* bigger than the other's!

Yet thanks to the miracle of the stock market, I—and some of you reading this—have been hugely benefited by Amazon as shareholders. And most all of us have been served by its trusted business, one that serves our nation and the world every day.

In May 2023, a Harvard|CAPS Harris poll asked U.S. Americans which institutions we trust the most. Coming in at #2 was the U.S. military, trusted by a large majority (77%) of Americans. Grading out slightly higher, as *the most trusted institution* in the lives of Americans today, was Amazon—at 78% (more than twice Congress's approval rating).

Excelsior.

It's easy to lose sight of this in a world where headlines are engineered to make you doom-scroll, and financial pundits obsess over the next crash, predicting "nine of the last five recessions," as economist Paul Samuelson once wrote.

When you ever find yourself doubting, just look at the stock market's graph over any long-term period: lower-left to upper-right. Even the big downturns—the Great Depression of the 1930s, the Great Recession of 2008–09—with all their attendant pain and fear, now show up as mere blips on the graph. You have to squint to see them.

Excelsior is not by happenstance. It is the worldwide accretion, generation after generation, of hard work and innovative thinking, most of all from the private sector. That people today—or any day—doubt this will persist is why Rule Breaker Investing is so lucrative. Part of me wishes everyone knew what Matt Ridley reveals in *The Rational Optimist*: that every era thought things would get worse, that the world might be doomed. "There is seduction in apocalyptic thinking," the late Eric Zencey once wrote. "If one lives in the Last Days, one's actions, one's very life, take on historical meaning and no small measure of poignance."

Instead, we should live forward with confidence and love, rather than fear and worry.

Still, part of me accepts that if fear is the tone the media or the next generation wants to set, it only helps build the Wall of Worry that, generation after generation, has enabled stocks—and especially, the Rule Breakers—to climb and climb again, to heights unparalleled.

To quote the British historian Thomas Babington Macaulay, "On what principle is it that with nothing but improvement behind us, we are to expect nothing but deterioration before us?"

EXCELSIOR.

THERE IS ANOTHER...

"A fool, a fool, I met a fool i' the forest,
A motley fool."

—WM. SHAKESPEARE,
AS YOU LIKE IT **[ACT II, SCENE VII]**

S HAKESPEARE EXPRESSED IT BEST, but Foolishness predates the Bard by millions of years. Ever since the first hominid challenged received truths, Foolishness was born on planet Earth.

The discovery of how to create and control fire is one of humanity's most significant achievements, believed to have occurred 1.5 to 2 million years ago with *Homo erectus*. I'm thinking the first Fool emerged in a society where tradition and authority reigned supreme, probably in a tribal setting. We shall call her Amara, an early human living in a small group dependent on natural fires, such as those started by lightning, in order to cook food and stay warm.

One day, observing the charred remains of a lightning-struck tree, Amara wondered: Could fire be replicated intentionally, instead of waiting for nature? The concept was unheard of, even taboo. Fire was revered, feared—a potent force of nature. But Amara had noticed that friction between certain materials produced heat and even sparks. No one had thought of this, dismissing such efforts as dangerous (or *foolish*). Or arrogant. Playing god.

Amara persisted.

After days of gathering dry leaves and bark, experimenting with rocks and sticks, and scraping her hands raw, Amara finally caught the faintest wisp of smoke. Ignoring the blisters and the ache in her muscles, she leaned in and blew gently—*fwoooosh*—feeding the ember, until it blossomed into flame. Against all odds, she had done it.

The tribal elders watched in awe as Amara kindled history's first controlled fire. Her discovery transformed her group's way of life, enabling them now to cook food and fend off threats. It also marked a pivotal moment in human history: One brave Fool had defied conventional wisdom. As a consequence, humanity's spirit of innovation and collaboration would carry this newfound knowledge forward, lighting the path to absolutely astounding future progress.

Maybe that's how it happened?

Or... maybe it was a longer time ago, in a galaxy far, far away....

WHO IS THE TRUE FOOL IN *STAR WARS*?

Shakespeare's Fools are my favorite characters in his plays; they are truth tellers with sharp wits, who hold up a mirror to the monarch. We named our company in celebration of these court jesters, the only members of court allowed to speak truth to power. And they were humble, too. The Fool never seeks to become King or Queen. The Fool is just a Fool, nothing less, nothing more.

In many ways, the Fools of Shakespeare find their echoes in the unexpected wisdom and humor found in certain characters of modern stories. For instance:

Who is the most Foolish character—the true Fool—in *Star Wars*?

There's a strong case for C-3PO. He's funny, ever-honest, and not afraid to deliver inconvenient truths (like calmly calculating the infinitesimal odds of survival, mid-crisis, for Han Solo). Plus, he has a British accent, reminding us of Shakespearean tongues. C-3PO may be the Fool...

... or is it R2-D2? Integral to providing advice and solutions at key points in the plot, R2 is certainly humble—without a voice, yet *speaking up* exactly when it matters most. Queen-like Leia trusts him with her hologram for Obi-Wan Kenobi. We enjoy R2-D2 puttering around the sets in that unassuming, Foolish manner of his—mostly confined to wheels (though he can show off rocket boosters to climb stairs, in a pinch!). Kids connect well with R2-D2.

Either character is a strong choice, and I can be argued into it.

Ah, but my pick for the Fooliest Fool in Star Wars is Yoda. Of the three, Yoda most clearly embodies wisdom. He's tiny, unprepossessing, and speaks in a funny way that makes kids laugh, simultaneously conveying a gravitas that commands adults' attention.

If you were a King or Queen, which of these three would you choose as your advisor? For me, YODA!

Which leads to my favorite line from the *Star Wars* saga, delivered by its greatest Fool.[106] You may already recognize it, but let me set this up anyway.

I told family and friends this would be "my final stock market book." In one sense, I expect that's true. Though as fully invested today as ever I was, my days are no longer focused on picking stocks. Thus, even despite cutting out more talking points than those I actually fit into this book(!), I think this is my final stock market book.

But looked at another way, I believe I have one more investing book in me.

Between these covers, I have set down my Six Habits, my Six Traits, and Six Principles. Yet, in the process of sharing these with you, I've recognized a fourth Six list.

The Six Steps to Breaking the Rules.

Breaking the rules has been essential to my investment success, and I hope it will be for yours, too.

---

106   Coming in at a close second, is Obi-Wan Kenobi: "Who is more foolish, the fool or the fool who follows him?"

But breaking the rules doesn't just help you win the game of investing. And that's not the only game I care about, anyway, not nearly. For ten years now, my weekly podcast has spent just one-third of its time on investing, a third on business (and your professional success), and a third on life. These are the three games I play to win, and I'm not satisfied with winning only one or two of them.

I've come to believe that breaking the rules, in the best sense— knowing how *and* when to break them—is the key to winning all three. For I believe that:

What wins in investing, wins in business, wins in life.

So if you're willing to suffer this Fool gladly once more... mayhap we call it a "Grand Unification Theory of Breaking the Rules"...?

"There is another...."

THINGS TO REMEMBER

6 Habits, 6 Traits, 6 Principles.

Trading is the antithesis of investing. *Investire*—keep that jersey on!

The stock market always goes down faster than it goes
up, but it always goes up more than it goes down.

Dips wait for dips.

I try to find excellence, buy excellence, and add to excellence
over time. I sell mediocrity. That's how I invest.

Dark clouds we can see through.

Throw good money after good! *Winners win.*

The Snap Test: "Would anyone notice?
Would anyone care?" *Snap Cola.*

Would you proudly wear the T-shirt of every
company you're invested in?

There are no numbers for the things that matter most.

The joy of investment gains is potentially
infinite times the pain of loss!

Buying in thirds.

Your sleep number!

Back your thoroughbreds and retire your also-rans.

When you find a better place for your money, put it there.

"Whether you think you can, or whether you
think you cannot, you're right."

"If you read today's headlines, you'll conclude things
have never been worse. But if you read history, you'll
conclude things have never been better."

Spiffy-pop.

What wins in investing, wins in business, wins in life....

RULE BREAKER INVESTING GLOSSARY

100-bagger—Are you an investor? If so, you can make a 100-bagger. You should. It's worth it. See also **baggers**; **investor**.

accuracy—Whether a stock pick beats the market's return (measured by the S&P 500). If it beats the market, it's accurate; if not, it's inaccurate. Your overall accuracy is the percentage of your total stock picks that are beating the market. Aiming for strong accuracy (60%+) helps Rule Breaker investors hold ourselves to a higher standard—shunning weak-sauce picks and keeping the bar elevated for our investment decisions.

Add Up, Don't *Double Down*—Rule Breaker Habit #2. Instead of throwing more money at struggling stocks (doubling down), add to your winners as they rise. This would have saved a *lot* of people a lot of money.

Amara—The first Rule Breaker?

anchor bias—The psychological tendency to fixate on an initial stock price or valuation.

back your thoroughbreds and retire your also-rans—I mean, I like this one, and I went with it in part because I needed to maintain my horse-racing analogy for about four different reasons. But "build your castles and abandon your ruins" might still win in a photo finish.

baggers (e.g., six-bagger, 10-bagger)—Originally coined by Peter Lynch, a "bagger" refers to a stock that has multiplied in value. Grabbed from baseball. A four-bagger is up 4x; a 10-bagger, 10x. Good news: A great stock racks up way more bases than a great hit. See also **100-bagger**; **baseball**.

baseball—Not just America's pastime—*Rule Breaker Investing*'s pastime, too. If you think I make too many baseball analogies, well...

you're probably right. But by now, you also know why: Home runs matter way more than strikeouts. A single stock can drive your entire portfolio's success, just like one grand slam can win a game. Babe Ruth struck out 1,330 times—but his home runs changed the sport forever. So go ahead, take your swings. See also **baggers; home runs vs. strikeouts**.

Bezos, Jeff—JB, have your people send my people the selfie! Thursday, September 13th, 2018.

buy discipline—What we're all about. A phrase you won't find in many investment books. See also **sell discipline**.

buy high and try not to sell—Our counterintuitive mantra: Great stocks often *look* expensive, but Rule Breaker investors benefit by holding through volatility rather than trying to time the market.

Buy Low Sell High—A tabletop board game designed by Reiner Knizia, published in 2005 and still available on Amazon. The only acceptable use of this phrase.

buying in thirds—Try it, you'll like it.

circle of competence (expanded definition)—A concept borrowed from Warren Buffett but Rule-Breaker-ized: your *best* investments aren't just within your expertise but within your best vision for the future. Also, ABE! (*Always Be Extending* your perimeter.)

Cola Test—Is this company so singular and/or dominant that you can find no Pepsi to its Coke? If so, you might have something special. See also **Snap Cola**.

compounding—Your portfolio's best friend. Don't interrupt it. Occurs in many areas besides money, like trust and relationships. A rich marriage, a gift to all those who surround it, is a beautiful example of compounding effects over time.

conscious capitalism—A form of capitalism that prioritizes purpose over profit—creating long-term value for customers, employees, society (shareholders too!). Rule Breakers seek out and invest in companies that embody it. See also **win-win-win**.

dark clouds you can see through—The market's convinced there's trouble; you see opportunity. When a stock is hammered by fear and you feel (confidently and dispassionately) you know better, your greatest investment returns may be just ahead. See also **"overvalued."**

Dead-Arm Initiative—A Foolish movement dedicated to preserving the English language and protecting "investing" from unnecessary adjectives; investing *by its very nature* is long term. If David ever utters the phrase "long-term investor/investing" in your presence, you have full permission to give him a dead-arm—a light but pointed knuckle-rap to the upper bicep. Better yet, start your own Dead-Arm Initiative! See also **investing vs. trading**; *investire*.

dips—... wait for dips. The common investor fallacy of waiting for a stock to drop, or drop *further*, before buying—often resulting in missing great opportunities.

excelsior—Latin for "ever higher." The personal motto (and motley) of the author and a core Rule Breaker mindset: embracing optimism and long-term upward trends in investing, business, and life. See also **motley**; **what wins in investing, wins in business, wins in life**.

every stock trades for $100 a share—A mental model for ignoring past price movements and focusing on a stock's current and future potential. See also **Peter Lynch**.

Faker Breaker—A stock masquerading convincingly as a Rule Breaker—flashy, exciting, disruptive—but ultimately lacking substance, vision, or staying power (usually missing Trait #4). Think MySpace, Napster, or more recently, Nikola. Beware of impostors.

Fool (capital F)—The only kind of Fool you want to be. A thinker, not a follower. An optimist, not a cynic. A Rule Breaker, not a rule taker. *"Who is the more Foolish, the Fool or the Fool who follows him?"* See also **Foolish investing**.

Foolish investing—Business-focused, rational investing as practiced by The Motley Fool since its debut as Ye Olde Printed Foole newsletter in July 1993—owning great companies, playing the long game. Best practiced with optimism, patience, and fellow Fools.

Gardner-Kretzmann Continuum (GKC)—A concept whose time has come—despite its elaborate name, it didn't take deep research or government grants to invent. An optional portfolio principle: Investors should own approximately the same number of stocks as their age.

Henrik's T-Shirt Test—A simple way to assess an investment, the brainchild of a German genius: *Would you proudly wear the T-shirt of this company?* A gut-check for alignment between your investments and your values.

home runs vs. strikeouts—In Rule Breaker investing, 10+-bagger home runs vastly outweigh all the strikeouts (bad stock picks), making risk-taking essential. "The least mentioned, biggest risk of all is not taking enough risk."

investing vs. trading—The Rule Breaker distinction: *Investing* is owning great businesses for years, even decades. *Trading* is short-term speculation. One builds wealth, the other churns fees and anxiety. *Are you an investor or a sunshine patriot?*

investire—The Latin root of "investing," meaning to clothe—but let's be real: It means putting on the jersey. When you invest, you suit up and take ownership. You wear the colors proudly because you believe in what you're backing and you don't switch teams on a losing streak. You stay in the game. See also **Henrik's T-Shirt Test; investing vs. trading**.

joy of investment gains—... is potentially infinite times the pain of loss.

losing to win—Some big losers are the cost of big winners. The key to Rule Breaker investing isn't avoiding failure—it's ensuring your best performers vastly outweigh your worst. As true in life as in investing. See also **joy of investment gains**.

macroeconomics—"Forming macro opinions or listening to the macro or market predictions of others is a waste of time." —Warren Buffett

Magnificent Seven score—Every few years, catchy names like "FAANG" or "Magnificent Seven" emerge to hype a handful of superstocks. Rather than chase the latest buzzword, Rule Breakers prefer tracking how long we've held these winners. Your Magnificent Seven score totals your years invested in Alphabet, Amazon, Apple, Meta Platforms, Microsoft, Nvidia, and Tesla. (Mine's 109 as of 2025—no Microsoft!) It ain't braggin' if it's true.

Make Your Portfolio Reflect Your Best Vision for Our Future—Rule Breaker Portfolio Principle #1. And like every #1 in this book, the most important.

motley—(1) A garment of mixed colors worn by a court jester. (2) The value you bring to work every day. A word, a phrase—what you most care about, aspire to, and define yourself by. How you choose to tell your story. *What's your motley?*

Motley Fool, The—An investing company accidentally started by David Gardner, Tom Gardner, and Erik Rydholm in 1993. It stuck around longer than they expected. See also **Fool**.

numbers—There are no numbers for the things that matter most.

optionality—The best Rule Breaker companies don't just win—they keep creating new opportunities for growth. "Go with the business that is opening up yet more options for itself."

"overvalued"—Market pundits' way of telling you a Rule Breaker is winning—dismissed, doubted, and deemed "too expensive"... right before it takes off. If they're saying it on CNBC, you're probably onto something.

"Person of the Year"—If it turns out you were right, you bought the stock, and it really was a Rule Breaker... give the CEO a decade. *Time* magazine will eventually catch up.

Peter Lynch—His book *One Up on Wall Street* is a Mount Rushmore investment great. Popularized and/or invented "baggers," "buy what you know," "don't water the weeds and cut the flowers," "every stock trades for $100 a share." Good guy, too.

rollercoaster—The stock market is the only rollercoaster where the ups and downs don't bring you back to where you started—but carry you far higher than you ever imagined.

Rowboat Syndrome—Most market participants are rowboaters, facing backwards, fixating over past prices. Credit for the analogy goes to Jack Bogle. I'll take associate producer credits for adding that traders are canoers, facing the right way but working too hard. Oh, and that part about the sailboat, too! See also **anchor bias**.

Rule Breaker—(1) Someone (you?) who thinks independently, embraces optimism, and backs the future rather than fears it. Plays the long game, breaks the right rules. Oh, and Rule Breakers have more fun! (2) A company or stock that meets most or all of our Six Traits from Part II.

sell discipline—Greatly overrated, this causes its adherents to interrupt their own compounding and trade too much, and yet—by invoking the phrase—still sound like *they're the ones who are the investment experts!* See also **buy discipline**.

sleep number—The max percentage you'll let a stock reach in your portfolio while still sleeping soundly at night. Investment genius discovered in the mattress aisle.

Snap Cola—A *Rule Breaker Investing* mnemonic for spotting the greatest stocks—those with a devastating one-two punch: They pass both the Snap Test and the Cola Test. See also **Cola Test**; **Snap Test**.

Snap Test—If you snapped your fingers and the company you're researching disappeared, would anyone notice? Would anyone really care? See also **Snap Cola**.

spiffy-pop—A holy grail moment of investing success: When a stock rises more in a single day than you originally paid for it. You never forget your first.

sports betting—One great big huge waste of money. Unless you're The House.

stocks always go down faster than they go up—... but they always go up more than they go down.

tech stock—A label applied so broadly and inconsistently it no longer has meaning. Used by financial media to oversimplify; avoided by Rule Breakers to clarify.

trading—Spending lots of time trying to make money maybe half the time.

truth—"Truth goes through three stages. First, it is ridiculed. Second, it is violently opposed. Third, it is accepted as self-evident." —Arthur Schopenhauer

View, The—Would be fun to close the loop on Starbucks. What say ye, producers?

what wins in investing, wins in business, wins in life—A framework in which I fervently believe. More anon.

win-win-win—The only truly ethical way to play the game of life. Real winners don't just win—they win-win-win, creating value for everyone. See also **conscious capitalism**.

winners—What *do* winners do...? (They win.)

You Get to Invest the Whole Race!—Rule Breaker Portfolio Principle #5. Unlike a horse race, where bets are placed before the race begins, investors get to add to their winners as they run. Yes, you can throw more money at Secretariat coming round the final bend!

RULE BREAKER INVESTING RESOURCES

EXPLORE ADDITIONAL RESOURCES for readers and fans of *Rule Breaker Investing*, including:

- A downloadable **bonus chapter**.
- A **discussion guide for book clubs & investment** clubs to explore and apply key ideas together.
- Curated lists of **top episodes from the Rule Breaker Investing podcast**, arranged by theme.

This and more available at:

rulebreakerinvesting.com

A portion of the proceeds of this book supports The Motley Fool Foundation, dedicated to helping people move from living paycheck to paycheck toward financial freedom. Learn more about our work at **foolfoundation.org**.

ACKNOWLEDGMENTS

IF YOU'RE READING THE ACKNOWLEDGMENTS, you're the kind of person who stays until the very end. I like you already.

This book, like any great Rule Breaker investment, is the product of time, compounding, and the contributions of many. First, my deepest loving thanks go to my wife, Margaret, and our three adult kids (Katherine, Gabe, and Zack), who have supported me every step of the way—not just in this book, but in the grander adventure of life.

To my father, Paul Gardner Jr., who introduced his kids to investing, setting me on this path long ago. His early lessons in patience and optimism planted seeds that have flourished into everything I do today. His good humor is irrepressible.

To Craig Pearce, my editor, who has been a steadfast partner in shaping this book from the get-go—pushing me when needed, reining me in when necessary, and always making this project better... maybe even "a page-turner"!

To my 18 beta readers, who generously gave their time and insights to refine these ideas before they reached the page. Your feedback was invaluable.

To the Rule Breaker Investing podcast community, who have kept the conversations vibrant and engaging for years. Your curiosity, enthusiasm, and thoughtful questions continue to inspire me.

To The Motley Fool and all my friends there, especially my brother and the analysts who dedicate themselves to serving our members with excellence and insight. I couldn't have asked for a better group of colleagues with whom to share this mission.

And finally, to you, the reader. Whether this is your first investing book or your 50th, I hope you walk away smarter, happier, and richer. Paraphrasing Marcel Proust, "The only true voyage of discovery consists not in seeking new landscapes but in having new eyes." May this book help you see investing—and your own potential—with fresh eyes and renewed conviction.

One Rule Breaker to another: Fool on!

David

ENDNOTES

INTRODUCTION

"That's a 3,370% increase, 34 times in value!"
"Dividend & Stock Split History," investor.starbucks.com, tinyurl.com/3hvhernn

CHAPTER 1

"But just realize if you *don't* make a habit of this rule, you'll never have the moon."
This is a Jason Robert Brown reference. Also rocking the same phrase, denigrating "risk-adjusted returns," see: "Risk-Adjust That Moonshot," fool.com (December 21, 2016).

"It's just that, for Rule Breaker investors like us, stock splits eventually give us incredibly low cost bases that have to be recalculated after years of holding."
For more information: www.fool.com/terms/s/stock-split

"On December 11, 2018, The Motley Fool ran a simple poll on Twitter/X with just one question and two possible answers."
tinyurl.com/4nbmv54b

"Near the end of my stock picking for The Motley Fool, I dedicated an entire podcast to drive this point home, aptly titled 'Losing to Win.'"
November 18, 2020, "Losing to Win": tinyurl.com/2pbp6can

CHAPTER 3

"We do need traders for market activity and liquidity, which allows equity investors today to enter and exit positions in one second—about 4,233,600 times faster than buying or selling a house."
According to a 2021 Ellie Mae Insight Report cited in *US News & World Report*. (Josephine Nesbit, "How Long Does It Take to Sell a House?" *US News & World Report* (June 28, 2024).)

CHAPTER 4

"That made a big impression on me when I first picked the stock at a split-adjusted price of 16 cents on September 8, 1997."
The original buy report lives for free forever on the internet: "The Rule Breaker Portfolio, Buy AMZN, September 08, 1997," www.tinyurl.com/36wa5vsz (September 8, 1997). Maybe that "16 cents" echoes with familiarity?

"Entitled '5 Stocks That Will Let You Eat Cake,' selected in November 2017..."
Search Google for "5 stocks that will let you eat cake" and we're the #1 search result! (How could we not be?) Hear it all at: tinyurl.com/3zaaufj4

CHAPTER 6

"Wall Street squeaked out a gain in 2007," the CNNMoney article started, "after what has been a particularly tough year."
Alexandra Twin, "Best and worst stocks of 2007," CNNMoney (December 31, 2007).

PART II

"*Rule Breakers, Rule Makers* was a hit, a bestseller."
David Gardner and Tom Gardner, *The Motley Fool's Rule Breakers, Rule Makers: The Foolish Guide To Picking Stocks* (Simon & Schuster, 1999).

CHAPTER 8

"When I ask Chick-fil-A restaurant operators what business they are in, none ever say 'fast food restaurant.' Instead, I hear responses like, 'We are a leadership academy masquerading as a fast food restaurant.'"
Ryan Jenkins, "Chick-fil-A's Secret Sauce for Attracting and Retaining Gen Z Workers," linkedin.com (April 30, 2020).

CHAPTER 13

"Buffett to Extend Aversion Toward Apple, Electronics Makers."
Jun Yang, "Buffett to Extend Aversion Toward Apple, Electronics Makers," Bloomberg (March 21, 2011).

CHAPTER 15

"I can't ride horses like she could,"
Corey Kilgannon, "And at the End, All the Comforts of the Carlyle," *The New York Times* (October 21, 2008), www.nytimes.com/2008/10/22/nyregion/22carlyle.html.

CHAPTER X

"In May 2023, a Harvard|CAPS Harris poll asked U.S. Americans which institutions we trust the most."
"The Harvard CAPS / Harris Poll," May 2023.

INDEX

Index

Index

R

Red Bull 91
research and development 140, 142
ResMed 90
resources 15, 239
return on innovation investment 142
Ridley, Matt 224
Robinhood 160
Rockefeller, John D. 87, 92
rollercoaster 6, 54–6, 70, 72, 80, 171, 237
Rosetta Stone 45
Rowboat Syndrome 31–3, 237
Rubinstein, David 218
Rule Breakers, Rule Makers 59, 85, 100, 112, 126
Ruth, George Herman "Babe" 34–5, 75, 234

S

Salesforce 95, 148
Samuelson, Paul 224
Schopenhauer, Arthur 92–3, 122, 145
Schultz, Howard 3, 119, 219
Sealey, Peter 130–1
See's Candies 165
sell discipline 44, 107, 194, 196, 237
Shakespeare, William 60, 173, 227–8
Shockwave Medical 191
Shopify 94, 115–16, 139, 148
Siegel, Jeremy 70
Sisodia, Raj 57
six-baggers 24
sizzle 47–8
sleep number 7, 185–92, 196, 205, 237
smart backing 119–27
Snap Cola Test 7, 94–6, 136, 238
Snap Test 58–61, 90–4, 167–8, 238
Sowell, Thomas 15–16
Spence, Roy 58
spiffy-pop 8, 155, 216, 232, 238
sports betting 198–9, 238
Spotify 93
Square 93
stakeholder orientation *see* win-win-win
Star Wars 228–9
Starbucks 3–5, 17, 61, 105, 119, 131, 219
stellar past price appreciation 107–17, 136
stocks always go down faster than they go up 70–1, 238

strikeouts 4, 34–8, 75, 236
strong consumer appeal 127–34
sunshine patriots 199–201
superhero movies 60–1, 105
supply and demand 16
sustainable competitive advantage 97–106, 140, 193
Syneron Medical 47

T

tech stock 238
Temple, William 122, 177–8
Tesla 17, 39–40, 59, 88–9, 95, 100, 111, 145, 149, 164–5
Thiel, Karl 116
thirds, buying in 181–4, 191, 234
three-year minimum 49–56
TikTok 130
time management 204–5
TiVo 45
Toffler, Alvin 131
toothpaste 130–2
top dog 58, 87–96, 124, 140
Trade Desk 139
traits of rule breaker stock 7, 24, 39, 85, 147–52, 155, 183, 189, 196, 229
    good management and smart backing 119–27
    "overvalued" 7, 18, 134, 135–46, 164–5, 237
    stellar past price appreciation 107–17, 136
    strong consumer appeal 127–34
    sustainable competitive advantage 97–106, 140, 193
    top dog and first mover 58, 87–96, 124, 140
Truman, Harry 221
truth 145, 238
T-Shirt Test *see* Henrik's T-Shirt Test
Twitter 36–7, 39, 144

U

Uber 101, 131
Ulrich, Dave and Wendy 130

V

Value Line 119
venture capitalists 77, 88, 97, 115, 126
View, The 1–5, 238
Voltaire 203, 209